90098

W9-CCS-331

WITHDRAWN

Kurtzman, Joel.

How the markets
  really work.

$18.95

BAKER & TAYLOR

PRAISE FOR HOW THE MARKETS REALLY WORK

"Kurtzman puts the profound and important truths about capital markets into a remarkably accessible package. He shows how prudent risk-taking by millions of investors makes access to capital more democratic for entrepreneurs with good ideas. More important, he makes it clear why this democratization of capital has turned the United States into a marvelous machine of job creation."

—MICHAEL MILKEN

"Joel Kurtzman places himself forward in time and provides a clear vision of the future of capitalism. Bravo."

—NEAL P. MILLER, portfolio manager,
Fidelity New Millennium Fund

"Kurtzman offers a clear, crisp, plain-English, example-laden treatment of why markets behave as they do—even irrationally. He explains where money comes from, why and how its supply grows and contracts, the risks of different investments, and myriad other aspects of the U.S. and global marketplace— always through the lens of the individual 'civilian investor.' He emphasizes the power of information and provides it in a readable, high content-per-page manner."

—PROFESSOR STEPHEN A. GREYSER,
Harvard Business School,
former editorial board chairman,
Harvard Business Review

OTHER BOOKS BY JOEL KURTZMAN

NONFICTION:

Radical E

Thought Leaders: Insights on the Future of Business

The Death of Money

The Decline and Crash of the American Economy

Futurecasting: Charting a Way to Your Future

The Soviet Union, Eastern Europe and the New International Economic Order (with Ervin Laszlo)

The Structure of the World Economy (with Ervin Laszlo)

Food for the World

World Leadership and the New International Economic Order

Europe and the New International Economic Order

The United States, Canada, and the New International Economic Order (with Ervin Laszlo)

Political and Institutional Issues of the New International Economic Order (with Ervin Laszlo)

No More Dying

FICTION:

Sweet Bobby

Crown of Flowers

CROWN BUSINESS BRIEFINGS SERIES TITLES

Bubbleology: The New Science of Stock Market Winners and Losers by Kevin Hassett

COMING SOON:

How Companies Lie: Why Enron Is Just the Tip of the Iceberg by A. Larry Elliott and Richard J. Schroth

The Myth of Market Share: Why Market Share Is the Fool's Gold of Business by Richard Miniter

Motivating the Front Line by Jon Katzenbach

The Morphing of Marketing by Larry Weber

Competitive Intelligence by Leonard Fuld

The Next Big Thing Is Really Small: Nanotechnology and the Future of Big Business by Jack Uldrich and Deb Newberry

HOW THE MARKETS
REALLY WORK

JOEL KURTZMAN

A CROWN BUSINESS
BRIEFINGS BOOK

CROWN
BUSINESS
NEW YORK

Published by Crown Business, New York, New York.
Member of the Crown Publishing Group, a division of
Random House, Inc.
www.randomhouse.com

CROWN BUSINESS is a trademark and the Rising Sun colophon
is a registered trademark of Random House, Inc.

Printed in the United States of America
Design by Meryl Sussman Levavi/Digitext

Library of Congress Cataloging-in-Publication Data
is available upon request.

ISBN 0-609-60965-3

10 9 8 7 6 5 4 3 2 1
First Edition

For Karen, Katie, and Eli

Contents

Introduction

A little over a decade ago, when the Soviet Union was in the midst of collapse, I wrote about the Evil Empire's economic demise for the *New York Times*. I recall very well one meeting in the winter of 1989 when a planeload of Soviet-style economists and politicians made their way to Chicago to the Kellogg School of Management at Northwestern University. The purpose of their visit was a closed-door discussion about markets with some of America's best thinkers from business and academia.

The oddest thing—aside from the baggy suits, shapeless dresses, and shell-shocked expressions worn by these Soviet-era apparatchiks—was how difficult it was for the American professors, business leaders, and government officials to explain the concept of how markets *really* work. Judging by the economic success of post-Soviet Russia—its economy is now one third as large as when the Soviet Union was in place—the message of the markets has yet to get through.

I suspect these befuddled Soviets were not the last people on earth for whom the markets held a measure of mystery. Many Americans do not really understand how markets—*and money*—work, either, despite the fact that more of their money is invested in mutual funds than deposited in banks and that nearly half of all Americans manage at least a portion of their own retirement savings by directly or indirectly investing in stocks, bonds, and other financial instruments.

The aim of this little book is to explain the *magic* of the markets and the thinking and machinery that make that magic work.

The idea that the markets are a highly coordinated dance of freewheeling uncoordinated dancers did not fly with these otherwise intelligent Soviets. The idea that the markets are a massive social mechanism for laying off some of the world's riskier bets was met with skepticism. In fact, when the subject of venture capital was raised, one gruff but influential director of a Soviet think tank asked where and for how long the founder of a failed start-up would be sentenced to jail. (The head of a major money-center bank quipped that the repossession of the founder's Porsche was punishment enough.)

These Soviets were people, after all, and for most people the size, role, mobility, and *importance* of the nation's and the world's capital markets are difficult to comprehend. The dance of money, and how the markets create wealth, is complicated. But it is also fascinating—as fascinating, in some ways, as the workings of the cell or gravity waves.

But what makes the markets even more fascinating is the fact that, unlike cells or gravity waves, markets are a creation of the human mind. They exist only because *we* made them and because *we* collectively use them. Markets are uniquely human—as uniquely human as the opposable thumb.

Also of interest is that while markets are vital to the functioning of most of the world's economies, and therefore responsible for the lives and livelihood of most of the world's people, they work without any central control.

True, markets have regulators as well as governmental and quasi-governmental participants, but they are, in essence, about as decentralized as anything on this planet can be. They are—as economists like to point out—*networks*. And we, the people and institutions that make up these networks, are merely nodes.

A network indeed! It is one that is massive, redundant, and highly robust. Consider its size and scope. The network of money and markets connects directly to about 300,000 computers situated on the world's professional traders' desks. Many of these computers, which are located in one physical location, have exact duplicates running in another location. The economic damage resulting from the attack on the World Trade Center was lessened because many firms, like Cantor Fitzgerald, had duplicate computers running in New Jersey and elsewhere. Charles Schwab's brokerage operation, for example, which is headquartered in earthquake-prone San Francisco, has a duplicate of all of its California-based servers running continuous backup in a number of eastern states. The New York Stock Exchange—a tremendously powerful node on the world's market network, to be sure—has exact duplicates of its Manhattan mainframes running continuously in an unmarked Brooklyn warehouse. These computers continuously hand off billions of operations from coast to coast, or from borough to borough, without losing a beat— *or a bit.* The technology of markets is amazing.

These dedicated trading systems are linked to another 25 million *or more* computers around the world inside large and small corporations and banks, via the Internet and various proprietary networks such as the highly secure banking networks named Society for Worldwide Interbank Financial Telecommunications (SWIFT), Clearing House Interbank Payment System (CHIPS), and Fedwire, that clear the nation's daily tally of one billion new checks and then move the money that must accompany each check so payments can be made. Each night, when the nation's check-clearing networks snap into action, money is moved electronically among more than 100 million checking accounts. As they do, money streams at nearly the speed of light to foot the bill for a myriad of grand plans and low-life follies. It also moves to cover shortfalls in the nation's twenty million margin accounts.

These buzzing, vibrant, massive networks are connected to others with as many as 300 million computers switching into and out of the world's money markets each day. As they do this, vast sums change hands—$2.2 trillion is moved electronically through the markets of New York City each day. How much is that? Every three and a half days, the entire gross domestic product of the United States—the measure of all we produce as a nation in a year—is funneled through New York.

Topics Covered

But how do these markets really work? What is their function? How do they affect our lives?

Despite their vast size, the functions of these markets are rather limited.

- They connect capital seeker with capital provider, thereby facilitating investment and the potential for gain and growth.
- Through auction mechanisms they discover prices for investments.
- They lay off present and future risk by pricing, selling, and distributing it as widely as possible.
- They locate price differences between markets and between present and future times and arbitrage between those differences.
- They provide ways in which claims can be staked on future wealth.
- They provide ways that debt can be packaged and sold.
- They connect financial institutions and create money.

Although this is all that markets do, it is how they do them that is fascinating and that this book will explore.

Every year, millions of people get involved in the stock market for the first time. Millions more are suddenly in charge of their pensions, 401(k)s, and other investment vehicles. When people enter the workforce for the first time, get raises, sell homes, or suddenly come into inheritances—as most of the Baby Boom generation is likely to do—they are suddenly confronted with one of the world's oldest questions: Where should I put my money? And why?

For the most part, their only sources for advice on this topic are restricted to investment books, brokers, and friends—all of whom have vested interests.

But thinking about dollar cost averaging or mutual funds versus individual stocks should not be the place to start. The place to start thinking about money is markets. By knowing how markets work and the instruments and vehicles that are traded on those markets, an investor becomes savvier. But where can someone turn to get that type of information?

This book is not about how to invest in markets. Rather, it is about how to *think* about markets. It is my contention that if people understand the magic of the markets, then they will become better magicians themselves.

The purpose of this book is to help people become market magicians.

CHAPTER ONE

What the Heck Are Prices, Anyway?

Let me try to answer a few of the most important questions my bedraggled old Soviets asked me way back when. They asked, If the world's financial markets are so important, what exactly do they do? And, why do they do what they do better than, say, government bureaucrats or computers or the KGB? How do the markets *really* work?

The answer to these questions is that financial markets don't really do all that much, it turns out, except provide capital to businesses, set prices, and distribute investment risk among a willing group of market participants.

They do what they do by bringing together interested buyers and sellers for various instruments like stocks and bonds in an organized fashion so those participants can haggle on-line, on the phone, or in each other's faces. Everything beyond that—from computerized clearing mechanisms to the bizarre hand signals used by the floor traders—is an add-on. Markets are places, real and virtual, to which market participants bring their money and their minds. In one form or another, people have been using markets since civilization began.

Providing capital is actually the easy part. No one can play the markets game without money or the ability to raise it. Players might come to the market individually, managing their own retirement accounts, or they might walk in with billions of dollars that they are paid to manage for other people. The slogan in the marketplace is the same as the slogan in the casinos of Las Vegas: "You got to pay to play."

Because so many people like the markets game, money has been rushing in to buy market-traded financial instruments. Most of that money used to reside inside the musty vaults and whizzy hard drives of banks, which dominated finance for hundreds of years, from the Middle Ages to the late 1980s. But the dominance of banks has been fading while the markets' star has been on the ascent. Money has been migrating from passbook accounts to the markets in pursuit of higher rates of return. In exchange for the opportunity of earning higher returns, investors have agreed to stomach significantly higher risk.

In the mid- to late '90s (no one knows the exact date, for sure) something changed with regard to how we manage our money. For the first time ever, people put more money into mutual funds than they had on deposit in their savings accounts. The trend to move money into the marketplace was not limited to the United States, although, as usual, Americans were a little less temperate than their counterparts in Europe and Asia when it came to diving into the markets. Trillions of dollars, marks, yen, and pounds flowed out of banks and into the markets everywhere. Even during the steep market corrections of 2000–2001, money continued to flow into the markets throughout that time.

During the last two decades or so, the amount of money invested in the financial markets globally has grown from about $2 trillion to about $20 trillion. In sync with that rise, the American markets grew from about $1.1 trillion to a high of about $13 trillion in 2000, before slipping back to about $11 trillion in 2001, when the markets tumbled. Eleven trillion dollars is a huge sum of money. It is equal to about one and a quarter times the value of all the work done by everyone in the United States and by every American company annually. Put another way, Americans have so much faith in the capital markets that they have invested in them the value-equivalent of more than a year's worth of all they make. Every day, a significant portion of that money (as much as a third!) changes hands as the prices for stocks, bonds, futures contracts—and everything else that is traded—gyrates up and down.

The world's financial markets are flush with cash and are expected to become richer still, growing as much as ten-fold in a decade's time. With so much money invested in the markets, there is plenty of capital available for companies. With so much capital available, parts of companies that at one time had little or no value can now be priced and sold, a phenomenon economists call the monetization of non-monetary assets.

Before the markets grew so large, the research and development and manufacturing arms of AT&T were considered overhead expenses—something the company needed to do in order to support its real business of providing long-distance telephone calls to its customers. But with cash flowing into the markets, AT&T could bundle, monetize, and sell those divisions, now called Lucent, in the stock market, thereby adding cash to AT&T's coffers while giving fledgling Lucent sufficient capital to invest in its growth.

Similarly, because of the growth of the capital markets, GM and Ford were able to sell to investors chunks of their captive parts suppliers. And because of the super-rich capital markets, dozens of not-yet-profitable (and maybe-never-profitable!) dot.coms and other early-stage Internet companies were able to raise cash by selling shares in the public markets. If you have enough cash, almost everything is for sale.

If the markets are a vast, global ocean bed, the amount of money in that ocean bed sets what economists call the price level. More cash means higher price levels (not necessarily for individual stocks) but for the market system as a whole. President Kennedy's famous quote about prosperity and the nation's poor—"A rising tide lifts all boats"—can also be applied to the causative relationship between money and prices. More money also means more items can be sold. If money is like an ocean, stocks, bonds, and other financial assets are like sponges designed to absorb the cash at hand.

To raise money in the markets, all a company has to do is go to a licensed underwriter—a Goldman Sachs, Salomon Brothers, Merrill Lynch, Credit Suisse First Boston, or any of the dozens of others—and ask them to sell shares, issue bonds, or sell some other product in the marketplace. From that standpoint, the individual markets are *reservoirs of capital* where money resides in its most *liquid* form (to keep the water analogies flowing). Companies want to sell shares—which are really ownership stakes—in markets that are rich, since that is where their chances are greatest of getting the highest price. Hence many European, Asian, and Latin American companies sell shares in New York, home of the world's largest and most cash-rich markets.

Liquid markets with lots of money and lots of participants offer big advantages to investors as well. Because so many people invest in those markets, in the blink of an eye, money invested in Microsoft shares can suddenly be freed to purchase shares in arch rival Oracle. Real estate, duck decoys, or handmade shotguns may at times see their value increase more than stocks, bonds, and futures contracts, but they change hands in markets that are far less liquid than markets for financial instruments. As a result, you might want to sell your duck decoy collection but be forced to wait months before you can find a qualified buyer. With financial instruments, a mouse click is usually sufficient to sell a stock instantly to a buyer who is waiting in the wings.

Creating financial offerings like stocks and bonds that will attract capital is the easy part, especially when the markets are brimming with loot. Setting a price for what is sold is where things get a little murky.

HOW PRICES ARE SET

Setting prices and sharing risks are more complicated undertakings than creating products because so little of what determines a price is under any single person's (or institution's) control. That is because prices are multi-level, multi-person, multi-organizational processes involving a host of different tangible and intangible elements all in a constant state of flux.

Price setting for individual products is a highly information-intensive, nerve-jangling business, far beyond the purview of computers. It is an act that is so complicated that when the old Cold War Soviets tried to do it for real-world goods (let alone financial instruments!) from a central office in Moscow, everything quickly got out of whack.

How much should you charge for a pair of decent shoes? It depends on the prices that you have to pay for labor, leather, shoelaces, dye, wax, tools, factory machines, energy, and rent. It also depends on how much money each shoe-making factory has to borrow (at what cost, for how long, and from whom), whether the workers have a share in the profits—*whether there are profits!*—and even whether the factory has to pay for the disposal of its waste and garbage and for its water and gas.

Then, if you are a shoe-price-setting bureaucrat somewhere in Moscow, you either have to determine the price for all the constituent goods that make up everything you use to make your shoes, from the price of petroleum to make dyes, to the price of beeswax to make polish, and so on down the line; or, if you cannot set those prices yourself, then you have to meet with your counterparts in the ministry of petroleum products and/or beeswax and work out a set of prices between you. But each of *those* prices is also dependent on other things, so all of the price-setting bureaucrats eventually have to meet to set prices together.

But once prices are set, what happens when the ministry of beeswax has to confront a bee-killing virus and must buy bees from abroad? And what happens when the ministry of petroleum needs money to invest in new wells because its old ones have run dry? Or when it has to buy new types of drilling tools and rigs from some other country at vastly raised prices?

As you can see, to do it right, price-setting bureaucrats must deal with a massive number of complexities. They also have to change their prices frequently to account for shifts in supply or demand and to take account of things such as weather. But that is not how governments work; they move methodically, infrequently, and at a glacial pace. As a result, in the old Evil Empire, some prices were not changed for decades, creating very odd situations where the final prices of almost all finished goods—railroad engines, jet transport airplanes, and, yes, even shoes—bore very little relationship to the cost of their production. Sometimes the components used to make a product cost far more than the price at which the government allowed the product to be sold. For that reason, there were huge shortages and long waiting times while factories sat idle until the government subsidies arrived to offset cash-flow problems caused by the government's price-setting ministries.

In those dark days (before Russia's current dark days), it took three to five years to have a car delivered even after the customer paid for it. To speed up the process, bureaucrats were often bribed. And when the car finally arrived, it might not have had all its parts, the result of shortages at the plant largely due to non-market pricing.

The culprit in the non-market system? Prices set by disinterested bureaucrats instead of interested buyers. (By *interested buyers,* I mean market participants with something to either gain or lose from a transaction.) Markets—where you have to pay to play—have no disinterested participants. Their function is to bring together people who want to get the better of each other.

By having only interested parties participating in the market, complexity is reduced. Shoe manufacturers can buy leather at on-line auctions when they need it and raise or lower the price of the shoes they make and sell depending upon their component parts and manufacturing costs and whether their shoes are in demand.

Similarly, rather than make centralized determinations regarding how much a share of Intel is worth, the market brings buyers and sellers together and lets them fight it out real-time. As a consequence, market prices for complicated items like stocks, bonds, and other financial instruments change constantly because everyone who is playing the game is also wagering a stake. As a result, they are forever jockeying to maximize their gains and minimize their risks.

Using the market to set prices and share risks is a very big deal. It is a big deal because prices for financial instruments are amalgams of lots of very different, very *human* ideas about the world. As a result, prices are unique forms of information. They are the way the myriad of participants that make up the market *collectively* view a financial instrument's performance and prospects.

Some of the information contained in a price is made up of so-called hard facts—a stock-issuing company's level of debt, rate of growth, and profit prospects, for example, or the stability and credit worthiness of a bond-issuing country or company.

But prices are also based upon soft information, like investor sentiment, mood, consumer confidence, and so on. Each additional item of hard or soft information is filtered through the millions of minds that make up the market. It is as if prices were determined not by any "wisdom central," but by the mob of people you encounter when you stand in line to get a new passport or a driver's license, some of them wise, some of them, well, not so wise.

The totality of what is considered by the financial market is a mix of everything from corporate reports and news to the opinions of other investors, the views of high-priced analysts, TV pundits, cabdrivers, and the chairman of the Fed. It is as if decisions changing the course of the markets were a meal containing everything from truffles and caviar to shoe leather and old socks. No two investors look at the same information in quite the same way, nor do they weigh their perceptions equally, nor do they have the same objectives or needs. Information rattling around inside one set of minds prompts that group to think it is time to sell. The same information buzzing around inside another set of minds says the time is ripe to buy.

Economists summarize the disparate elements that determine price most famously and glibly with their ultra-minimalist phrase "supply and demand." Taken together, the supply of goods, services, and other items like financial instruments and the demand for those same goods and services somehow yields price. In the minds of these economists, markets are machines for efficiently clearing *marketplaces* of their goods and services. Markets clear low-quality goods—and goods in vast abundance—by assigning to them lower prices, using some form of auction. They clear marketplaces of rare and precious goods and services by assigning them higher prices, also through some form of auction. In each instance, markets make it worth a seller's while to get rid of what they own or control and to do it quickly. In this way markets set prices.

But the perception of markets-as-machines doesn't do justice to all of the confusing human factors that go into determining demand and supply. Prices for instruments like stocks and bonds always depend upon a host—*a myriad, even*—of other things, besides supply and demand, such as how much money is available and in people's hands and in which market a good or service is sold.

Prices are conditional, dependent, and ultra-short-term with the factors that actually create a price coming together only *in the moment*. Prices for instruments like stocks and bonds depend not only upon supply and demand but also upon what people *think* about supply and demand. For that reason, prices swing like a pendulum rather than click like a hand on a clock. At one moment the swing undershoots on price, at another time it overshoots. A good stock with healthy demand is underpriced when sentiment about the future is fearful or people are out of cash. The same stock with the same fundamental prospects for the future is priced higher when sentiment is bright and people are flush. A pendulum swings through the middle, it never stops there.

Prices, like the Buddha's smile or the wind patterns on the desert sands, are fleeting. Tomorrow's prices will be set by factors different (or by the same factors in different proportions) from those that set prices today. They are like the famous river of change about which the ancient Greek philosopher Heraclitus said "into which we cannot step twice." The factors that influence today's prices are gone once the trigger is pulled and the trade is executed.

After a trade is made, the price of the latest transaction becomes a factor influencing the prices of all subsequent transactions. Like billions of big and little pebbles thrown at intervals into a placid lake, today's prices radiate outward and impinge—*in some way*—on the prices of every other instrument that is traded. As a result, prices, economists like to point out, are a type of information that is a rich summary of all we know and *feel* about a stock, bond, or other financial product along with all we know about its issuer and the issuer's prospects at any given moment in time. Also contained within that summary is the market's assessment of risk as well as its general assessment of the future of a market sector, a market, and the world.

That overall informational summary is what constitutes *price,* and its half-life is very short. It is a product of the mind, a construct, something we all must agree upon; it is not an absolute.

The trouble is, though, that while many people might know what is influencing prices at any moment, no one knows how each of those influences is weighted by the investor community as a whole.

But price is not value. Value is something different. Orthodox stock market mavens—those who follow Benjamin Graham, an influential investor and professor of business at Columbia University in the 1930s and '40s—view value as the sum of a company's cash flow throughout its lifetime, discounted back to the present. (Cash flow is revenue less certain expenses.) When value, measured that way, is less than a company's current share price, it is a signal to buy. When the price of a company's stock is higher than its measured value, it is a signal to sell. That's the way investors such as Warren Buffett view the market.

In practice, DCF, as the cognoscenti call discounted cash flow, is not, well, rocket science. It works in a pretty logical way—so much so that the worst you can say about it, when you are trying to implement it, is that it makes you a little drowsy. Investing should be exciting and fun. It should require bold strokes of intuition, flashes of brilliance, and moments of high anxiety as you wait for the market to vindicate your hunch. And yet, the world's greatest investor, Warren Buffett, is more in the green-eyeshades camp, employing a number-crunching formula that leads more to yawns than a state of awe. But consider the results!

Here's how you think about discounted cash flow. If money is buying power and inflation is rampant, today's money buys more than tomorrow's money. My mother was a movie buff. When she was young, in the 1940s, she paid less than one dollar for a ticket. At the time of this writing, tickets cost between seven and ten dollars. (Ouch!) In my son's day, it is certain that tickets will cost far more.

What this means is that my mother's dollar bought more than my dollar, but my dollar buys more than my son's. If inflation runs at 5 percent, an investment must pay greater than 5 percent in order to yield more buying power than when it started. Add to that taxes and the cost of the transaction, and you have to earn 9 or 10 percent just to make a profit in an environment with 5-percent inflation. To figure out whether an investment will continue to pay sufficiently so that future generations can go to the movies, you have to think in terms of the link between price and cash flow. For an investment to make sense, an investment (its cash flow and the underlying price you pay for that cash flow) has to exceed the damage done by inflation, taxes, and other transaction costs. As a result, long-term investors, like Buffett, are out to buy "cash flow" in the form of dividends that a company either gives to shareholders or reinvests. But while they are seeking cash flow, they also know that time has a discounting effect on that cash flow due to inflation and other factors.

DCF investors are long-term investors. As a result, they are less concerned with their paper gains—what a stock is selling for—over the medium term, than they are with how much it pays as dividends. As a result, they discount the money they invest today in a stock over the long haul and discount the dividends to see if the investment is worth it.

To get a sense of how DCF investors think, have a look at the following information on Boeing, from the good old days of 2000. The chart, from Val-U Investor's website, shows how DCF investors think.

Highlights

- Boeing's aircraft and missile division plans to reduce expenses by $1.5 billion this year, after cutting costs by $1 billion last year.
- The government's current plan is to increase the defense budget from $45 billion (in fiscal 1998) to $75 billion in 2005. Some of these increases will go toward the Apache Longbow program for the U.S. Army, a project that Boeing is currently working on.
- The company is starting to develop its own satellite systems and services. It recently won a contract to build satellites for the U.S. Military's imagery reconnaissance program. Though the details are classified, analysts estimate the contract's value to be around $5 billion through 2010. The aerospace industry predicts that satellite communications will generate annual revenues of $160 billion by the early 2000s.

Valuation

Boeing is a regular cash cow. The company has more than $3 billion in cash and generated about $2.85 billion in free cash flow for the year 2000. Based on estimated discounted free cash flow of $2.52/share (for 2000), an estimated price/free cash flow multiple of 24×, and an annual dividend of $.56/share, we give Boeing a 12-month price target of $61.

Never mind that at the time of this writing, eighteen months after the DCF analysis, Boeing shares, after briefly touching $60, had fallen to $35 a share. We will return to DCF later in this book.

Trouble is, markets don't always take value into account the way analysts and investors think they *should,* as the preceding chart suggests. There are many irrationalities in the market. Sometimes prices dive and sometimes they soar in ways that are out of whack with Graham's orthodoxy. The big stock market crash of October 19, 1987, when share prices fell by 22.6 percent in a single day, was not precipitated by a crisis in listed-company values; it was based upon a crisis in confidence. Similarly, though the stock market sell-off of 2000–2001 was fueled in part by the failure of many dot.coms to earn a profit, many of the traditional companies that were hurt did not experience any measurable changes in their Graham-defined value.

Over the years, when I have interviewed financial analysts, economists, and stock pickers, they almost never agreed on what *exactly* prompted a market sell-off or a rush to buy, though they usually agreed on what information was significant. More important, none of these market "experts" could forecast the future for very long. If you doubt what I say, all you have to do is retrieve and read a few issues of last year's *Wall Street Journal, Forbes, Business-Week,* or the *New York Times* and compare what the pundits said *then* to what they are saying *now.*

True, new information does affect the market, whether it is new information about the supply or demand for computer chips, potato chips, wood chips, or paper clips. But information never makes its way into the markets directly. Since there are no real prices until a trade is made, a release of data is really important only when it prompts someone to act by making a bid. A single item of news rarely does it. To make a trade, investors need stacks of data and heaps of information. Which item of information causes an investor to snap into action is anybody's guess. A million investors, a million diverging and converging opinions.

The run-up of technology stocks from the early 1990s until March 2000 was fueled, most agree, by the well-publicized growth in demand for computers and related technologies and services due to the growth of the Internet and to high-tech's positive effect on productivity. But when those stocks began to tumble, the demand forecasts for high-tech products and services barely budged. For some reason, the many millions of minds that make up the collective intelligence of the market changed the way they felt about those forecasts and the future. Instead of continuing to animate a collective sense of high-tech market exuberance, the mind-of-the-market turned grim.

Suddenly, the excitement, fun, and promise of the Internet party was only a dim memory, replaced by a bad morning-after headache. Once the room stopped spinning

and the toxins were emitted from the system, the sentiment on Wall Street was everywhere the same: "I promise I'll never do *that* again," the investor community
swore. But of course they will. The only question is *when*.

So what ended the great Internet party of '97–'01? Or
the biotech party before that? Or the personal computer
party before that? Or the oil and gas and conglomerate
party before that?

It ended, most of the world's hindsighted analysts
say, because rather than rising sales of high-tech and
related equipment and services, investors suddenly
demanded *profits*. But what exactly caused the shift—*and
why it shifted when it did*—is anybody's guess. While we
can all speculate—and theories abound—the truth is that
no one knows for sure what caused the shift and why it
happened when it did. No one knows which new *straw* of
information broke the market's back.

With the movement away from the Internet, the markets gave short shrift to hundreds of companies and their
leaders. Those who could do no wrong could suddenly do
no right, and the prices of many high-flying firms crashed
into the earth. And yet, though trillions of dollars were
lost by investors as the markets slid, trillions of dollars
more ($11.2 trillion in CDs and money market accounts,
as of 2001) waited, ready to party on when the next invi-
tation arrives.

Economists say that prices, because they are such
complicated patterns of information, are really only "discovered" at the moment the parties agree to a sale and that
the only real "test" of a price is whether it receives a bid
and the only real test of a bid is whether it is accepted.
Since there are no disinterested parties in the market,

everything aside from an accepted bid is either posturing blathering or a little of both.

In some ways, selling stocks is not very different from auctioning off paintings by Picasso or Rembrandt or antique cars by Bugatti. The cognoscenti may say a Rembrandt is worth X or even double or triple X (just like analysts say a share of stock should be worth Y) but no one knows for sure until the gavel goes down (or the last mouse click is heard). That is the only time anyone really knows how much a Rembrandt or a Bugatti is worth.

The same is true with stocks, bonds, and other financial instruments, except that rather than selling one or perhaps two Rembrandts a year, each day on the New York Stock Exchange, to name only one market where stocks are traded, billions of shares worth trillions of dollars are traded.

The amount of information—and the rich array of assumptions—in the daily price fluctuations of the stocks listed on the NYSE is truly dazzling. There is enough information circulating the globe to enable the NYSE's millions of participants to revise their assumptions on a minute-by-minute basis, which is why prices often change with such force and suddenness.

So, how much is a share of stock or a bond or some other financial instrument really worth? It all depends on *when* you ask the question. Prices are situational. In the price prediction business, no one always *knows* and no one always *wins*. In the price prediction business, no one ever knows for sure which type of information—hard or soft—dominates.

CHAPTER TWO

Three Cheers for Volatility

Though I cannot prove it beyond a reasonable doubt (I take comfort from the fact that no one else can, either), I will make an assertion: The rise in market volatility is closely linked to the increased use of computers and the Internet on the trading floor, at brokerage houses, and at home.

I believe that the markets are moving more erratically, faster, and more unpredictably due to the torrent of information that is reaching investors. Since prices are a type of information, they are bruised, bolstered, and buffeted by the massive flow of other types of information making its way through the investor community. Increased volatility is also a function of the ease with which transactions can be executed now that we are all on-line with devices ranging from mainframes to a myriad of "palm" devices. By electronically linking millions of human brains to the market—*and focusing their attention on its ups and downs*—

the markets now resemble a giant central nervous system, and I emphasize the word *nervous*.

For the uninitiated, market volatility is the aggregate movement of prices over any measured term—daily, weekly, monthly, or annually. And, while a volatile market can still be an upward- or downward-moving market over the long haul, it makes those moves in fits and starts. Today, almost all of the world's financial markets (stock, bonds, futures, currencies, and their derivatives) have become more volatile and the rate of volatility is increasing.

If you hold financial instruments over the long haul, volatility makes no difference to you. A long-term investor really only needs to think about the market's overall direction. But if you hold positions for shorter periods—or need to sell an instrument in a hurry to raise cash—price volatility can present you with problems and opportunities. Indeed, an entire community of people called electronic day traders has emerged to try to take advantage of daily market fluctuations, with various degrees of success.

When computers first made their way onto the trading floor of the New York Stock Exchange in 1971, they were used chiefly to clear the market of a day's worth of trades by matching buy-and-sell orders, a task previously accomplished by hand. By performing these matches electronically, the big, hulking computers of yesteryear increased the speed at which transactions could be processed. This in turn made it easier for sellers to get cash. With money in their pockets, sellers could become buyers and reenter the market more quickly.

A few years later, in the mid-'70s, computers began

making their way into the world's brokerage houses. In the beginning, there were a few mainframes made by IBM and a few other companies that are now, for the most part, defunct. Compared to today, these machines put the processing power of a slide rule on each trader's desk. Using computers, traders figured out buy-sell spreads and interest rates, computed prices, determined gains, and aggregated orders that were then sent to the trading floor via a primitive type of e-mail. On the floor orders were executed by hand.

In the late '70s, in the days of the Carter White House and the song "Stayin' Alive," something very big happened. Reuters, the news-gathering organization, began leasing computer terminals to brokerage houses. These terminals not only displayed real-time information on currency prices, globally—*a first*—but they were also linked directly to the markets so currency dealers could swap currencies and related instruments electronically. Along with their buy-and-sell capabilities, traders could read breaking news—courtesy of Reuters' global news service.

Breaking news sent to brokerage firms was not something new. In some houses, there were "wires" that printed out news stories along with stock prices on the ticker tape. There were telephones, of course, so one broker could call another with a rumor, a joke, or a lie, and there were newspapers, newsletters, radio, and later TV.

But Reuters changed trading very dramatically. Before Reuters, there were only centralized news sources, aside from the telephone. A news feed or stack of newspapers would go to some central place in the brokerage house to be distributed *whenever* to *whomever.* It came when it came, usually long after the news actually happened. When Reuters made its way into the trading room, news from an important and reliable source was suddenly—and literally—*within reach.*

Putting news on a trader's desk meant that it received attention, and in the grand scheme of things, attention leads to action. Rather than *reflect* on events, traders were suddenly prompted to *react* to events. They did so because they realized that their colleagues and competitors, armed with the same information at the same time, would also try to act on that information in an effort to gain the upper hand. It was what scientists who study systems call a self-reinforcing loop and with it, the market's electronic central nervous system began taking shape.

Oddly, that nervous system does not seem to care whether the information it receives is actually true. It does care if it is believable and it also cares how many other people see it and believe it. From the market's standpoint, the test is whether or not people will act on the information they receive, not whether it is true beyond a doubt.

I learned that in an interview with one of the top economists on Wall Street. His job was to forecast shifts in the economy, project interest rates, and figure out the direction of the markets. He worked for a global insurance company with a diversified portfolio worth many billions of dollars that was invested around the world.

During a particularly volatile period in the nation's economic history, I asked him about a just-issued report from the Commerce Department saying that the nation's gross domestic product—the sum total of all it produces—grew by 1.4 percent in the previous quarter. Because it is difficult to gather data, the Commerce Department issues corrections a few weeks or even months after its initial release. In turbulent times, the first data release is not considered to be terribly accurate.

Even so, this economist told me, nearly every Wall Street economist and analyst acted *as if* the data was accurate, though they knew it was flawed. Sometimes the data was off by as much as a plus or minus sign, but the average error was 1.4 percentage points up or down. What that meant was that if these numbers were off by the average amount of error, no one would be able to tell if the economy was dead in its tracks or growing robustly.

Yet, Wall Street analysts and economists always talked to the media, advised clients and people inside their firms *as if* this flawed data were true. They did so, he said, because everyone else was doing it, too. If everyone (with few exceptions) in the investment community was acting as if the economy was growing at a sustainable rate (based on data they all knew to be inaccurate), then you also had to act as if that dubious fact were true.

"One thing I learned on Wall Street," this economist said, "was that you can't go against what the market thinks even if what the market thinks is wrong."

And because it is a *wired* market, its participants tend to think the same thing at the same time.

In the late '70s, when minicomputers were introduced (a few years ahead of PCs), trading houses were suddenly able to put a lot more processing power to work not only to figure out spreads and do simple math, but to do analysis, too.

In the late '60s, Harry Markowitz did work for which he later won a Nobel Prize in economics. In his studies, he analyzed hundreds of stocks to figure out mathematically how to build portfolios to manage market risk. At the time, it took Markowitz hours of computer time, costing thousands of dollars, to build a single portfolio of about thirty-five stocks—far too expensive and slow for anyone but a few fund managers to use.

With the advent of minicomputers, and later PCs, Markowitz's equations not only became fast—a few seconds versus many hours—cheap (try free!), and easy to run, they also became almost ubiquitous. By the early '90s, Markowitz's mathematical models were being sold as software on floppies to PC users in the back pages of *Money* magazine. So widespread was the dissemination of his work that the early advantages of its use were largely lost by the fact that so many funds and so many people were using it. What was esoteric in the '60s became commonplace.

The same was true for a number of other computerized market innovations. Fisher Black and Myron Scholes, who won a Nobel Prize for figuring out ways to price an option to purchase a stock at a future date, had their work turned into software that was put into use by nearly every trading house and almost all major companies in the world. The same was the case with Nobel laureate Merton Miller and many other once-arcane economists, whose work focused on the markets, risk, portfolio building, and investment strategy.

With computers moving onto Wall Street, the environment began to shift from one in which family connections and a good haircut got you a job, to one in which high scores on the math portion of the SAT were what counted.

Even so, making the markets technological did not happen overnight. On October 19, 1987, when the stock market suffered its largest daily collapse ever, Charles Schwab, chairman of the big discount broker that bears his name, complained to me in an interview that he did not have enough people available to verify the volume of on-line transactions his firm received.

Back then, in the technological equivalent of the Pleistocene age, an on-line order had to be verified by a person in the brokerage house before a trade could be made. With too few people to verify orders at Charles Schwab & Company and at the other on-line brokerage firms, a backlog developed. Tens of thousands of people wanting to buy and tens of thousands of people wanting to sell had no way of meeting in the middle, with respect to price. Without knowing who wanted to buy or sell, the market's middlemen, called specialists, were unable to determine whether they should dump their holdings or buy more to prevent wild price swings. Without mechanisms for matching buy and sell offers, prices could not be discovered. The market fell into disarray for many hours. But for many investors, it took days to discover how much they made or lost.

After the '87 crash, the rules were changed to allow people with electronic access to their brokerage accounts to enter buy and sell orders directly into the computer their firms used to execute trades, thereby eliminating a bottleneck. Without the need for human intervention, a broker's computers can aggregate buy or sell orders and send them to the appropriate exchanges where they are matched and priced, so transactions are completed, often through the auspices of specialists. And, while people still oversee the *operations,* they do not necessarily oversee each individual trade unless those trades are for very large blocks of shares or are executed after normal trading hours.

Today, with computers and palm and cell devices locked in a micro-electronic, Internet-enabled embrace, and with TV, radio, and print also focused on the market, finance is everywhere. And, whereas total market capitalization has grown ten-fold in the last twenty years, the amount of information available on the markets has grown by at least that much, perhaps more. We are inundated with market and business news. No wonder that trading volume has increased so dramatically, from 604 million shares traded on the NYSE on Black Monday (a record at the time), to more than a billion and a quarter shares traded there on an average day in 2001.

Prices are a unique form of *discovered* information, wrapped in an ever-growing cloud of information about them and about the markets in general. As a result, giving hundreds of millions of investors—from Wall Street professionals to back-street amateurs—direct and constant access to such a vast supply of information can lead to overload from time to time or outright confusion. Reason still predominates, as much as it ever has, but reason can be overwhelmed by the sheer volume of news that is so often contradictory.

I do not think people's propensity to buy or sell stocks or any other financial product has probably changed very much over time. Neither has their tolerance for risk. People who study human behavior seem to agree. What has changed are the tools people have at hand to act on what they think and feel. Let me give you an example of what I mean.

For a research project I was involved in when I was the editor of the *Harvard Business Review,* I once interviewed a man who began his career as a stockbroker on Wall Street shortly before the stock market crash of 1929. He told me that in the days of Mary Pickford, the Charleston, and Pierce-Arrow automobiles—when RCA was a high-flying high-tech stock (it made radios, after all)—people liked to take an active hand in managing their investments. Back then, what differed most, he said, was the world's communications infrastructure and an individual's ability to transact business.

In those days, when his clients traveled to Europe from the United States, it was common for them to sell all of their stock before departing and to put the proceeds in the bank.

They sold their holdings because getting information about a company or the market was not easy unless you could talk to your broker directly. Radio carried almost no news about the economy, general interest newspapers did not have business sections, and only a few specialty newspapers carried any financial information at all. *Fortune,* one of the first business magazines, did not even begin publishing until 1929. Financial information was in the possession of only a select group of people.

In addition, if you were in Europe, you could not call your broker directly. If you wanted to, you had to place a call through an operator and before you could do so, you had to reserve a time for that call. And it was expensive.

If you called your brokerage house to get information, you could get information that was somewhat current through the ticker tape, and if you wanted to execute a trade, your broker would have to call his trading office in New York, which would in turn call the floor traders, who would gather up all of their trades in a particular stock and execute them at once. (If you could not book a call, you could send a telegram and then wait many hours or a day for a reply.) The point is that the time delay was so great, you had no certainty regarding whether and when your trade had been made, not to mention at what price.

Primitive communications meant that it did not take much buy-and-sell volume to overwhelm the trading system. When the markets rose in the early '20s, they did so largely because information about good investment opportunities traveled by word of mouth and most of that transmission happened face to face since telephones were relatively rare and the lines were often crowded. Just like now, good news about a rapidly growing economy (automobile sales went from a few thousand just prior to the onset of World War I, in 1914, to more than three million in 1929) translated into a rising market flush with cash. But when the stock market crashed, a little more than a year after my interviewee made his way onto Wall Street, pessimism about the markets remained in place for a decade.

People were pessimistic for a number of very *rational* reasons. Less money was available to invest and the banking system was in shambles, thanks to a moralistic and largely inexperienced Federal Reserve Board (it was created in 1913) that did not really understand how to pull the levers of the economy. With far too little money in circulation, and virtually no credit available, the economy plunged into a downward spiral culminating in the Great Depression. Adding to this, my informant said, there was no way to get out the word when a new opportunity arose. As such, the cloud of economic pessimism and despair that hung over the country and much of the world could not be dispelled by new information. Investor sentiment hovered at the level of nervous pessimism and occasionally rallied to the level of confident gloom. Today, with CNBC, CNNfn, Bloomberg TV, and a plethora of other services, including Reuters, news of an opportunity can spread at the speed of light.

While the downside of linking hundreds of millions

of investors with one another and of gigantic flows of financial information has been greater market volatility, the upside has been tremendous growth in the size of the markets accompanied by far less volatility in the so-called *real* economy.

The real economy is the area of our lives where people create services and products and deliver them to each other. The real economy is where computers are made, food is grown, and products are moved from town to town. It is the domain of airplanes, railroads, houses, cars, and consultants. The real economy is where most of us work. The financial economy—which is the domain of the markets—is where the real economy is financed. But it is also the area of our lives where money and financial products are traded for the sake of speculation. Though it employs far fewer people than the real economy, the financial economy is several times larger than the real economy when measured from the standpoint of transaction volume.

Since the end of World War II, the frequency and severity of recessions per decade affecting the country has gone from two long, deep recessions in the '50s, to two moderate recessions in the '60s, to one and a half deep, long recessions in the '70s (I'm crediting the '70s with one and a half recessions because the 1970 recession was really a spill-over from the late '60s), to two recessions in the '80s (one moderate and one deep), to one short, shallow recession at the very beginning of the '90s.

One explanation for the remarkable "smoothing out" of the nation's growth trajectory—and the accompanying increase in volatility of the financial economy—has been the increasing level of skill with which the Federal Reserve Board manages its affairs.

In addition to the Fed's newfound mastery, there is the way in which information travels from terminal to terminal, from device to device, in ways that were unheard of before the advent of the silicon chip.

If one reason for pessimism to persist in the '30s was because there were too few connections between people to communicate dynamic new opportunities, the myriad of information and connections available today makes it easy to put capital to work. Positive new developments in the real economy rarely go hungry for funds. In fact, one reason for the run-up of technology stocks during the '90s was the tremendous supply of money chasing after each new public offering of stock. With so much money available—and so much information existent—investors funded the economy's future as well as a few of its follies. Armed with libraries of print and on-line information about nearly every company and the way each is managed, the markets continued to shovel money at the topmost performers.

Brilliantly run companies like GE, Microsoft, Intel, Berkshire Hathaway, Home Depot, and others were rewarded with an unlimited supply of capital from an appreciative and informed investor community, which sent their stock prices up and their borrowing costs down. Using their stock as a highly prized, highly valued form of currency, the leaders of these companies acquired other companies, which put more and more of the nation's resources under the control of its best business minds. With more of the economy run by this business elite, the overall economic picture improved. Big, well-managed companies became customers not only for products and services produced by a legion of start-ups, they also became customers for the start-ups themselves. The best start-ups either flourished on their own or joined large, well-run corporations.

Information, combined with capital and a distributed and informed investor community, changed the way the economy works. Rather than long periods of bearish sentiment, followed by a slow awakening into a world of new possibility, the growth of the capital markets has meant that a virtuous cycle now exists whereby good performance is rewarded by higher levels of capitalization, which enables the best performers to extend their reach further. Because capital is widely distributed among individual investors and a host of professionally managed funds, risk can be parceled out among a larger group of participants.

At the same time, the growth of the electronic nervous system has meant that downturns—which will never be banished altogether—tend to last for shorter periods of time. This is true globally, and is likely to be true domestically as well.

Take, for example, the meltdown of the Asian economies (excluding Japan), which began in late 1997 and was over in 1999. During that time, stock markets collapsed, currencies plunged, and companies died. A number of economists forecast that a depression would grip the region. Others speculated that the grim problems of the region would work their way to Europe and America in what was being called the "Asian Contagion."

But rather than an Asian Contagion, something else occurred. Informed investors, stuffed with on-line analyses and reams of information, saw the crisis as an opportunity for them to invest. The investor community did not run from Asia into the supposed safe havens of gold, U.S. Treasury bills, and Miami real estate. Instead, they ran *to*

Asia, and invested capital in an area with some temporarily troubled assets but huge potential. Strategic investors like Ford, GM, and Renault came to buy larger shares in companies they already knew. Financial investors came to buy stocks and other financial instruments at fire-sale prices.

Rather than a depression, Asia experienced a quick rebound, prompting economists to speculate that while historically most downturns are U shaped, meaning values fall to hug the bottom before prices rebound, downturns are now beginning to be V shaped, where a rapid fall is followed by a rapid rise.

I personally believe in the V-shaped view of the markets for two reasons. The first is that computers and the ability to react quickly to events have made investors better able to move money where it is needed at the very moment the time is ripe.

The second reason I believe in the V-shaped downturn is because volatility is really a double-edged sword. Yes, volatility means that we are much more likely to experience sharp dips due to swift changes in investor sentiment. These changes in sentiment can sweep through the world's electronic central nervous system in seconds, wreaking havoc on markets. But swift downs can also be followed by swift ups for the very same reasons. As such, volatility may make the ride up the hill jerky, but the direction remains the same. And, while the ride may make some queasy, it has done wonders for those of us toiling in the real economy, down below. For those of us working in fields of commerce (other than finance), capital has never been in more abundant supply. And if the price to be paid for all that capital is a case of the jitters every once in a while, so be it!

CHAPTER THREE

The Secret Life of Money

Some time ago, I wrote a book about money and the emerging electronic markets. During that exercise I had occasion to discuss the topic of money with economists and traders around the world and with a number of very wealthy investors. When I asked each of them about the nature of money, I was always surprised to learn that none of them really cared. They said that as investors, their game was to amass as much buying power as they could using all of their skills. They reasoned that they wanted as much money as possible along with all of the goodies it could buy. As long as money was to buying power what batteries were to electricity, that was good enough for them. They did not care very much about its nature. And yet, from my perspective, understanding the nature of what you are trying to obtain comes in handy when you are attempting to get it, which is what this chapter is about.

Although dollars resemble batteries charged with a standardized unit of buying power, dollars differ from batteries in that electricity exists in nature and money is entirely a product of human creativity. As far as we know, no other inhabitants of this planet use money or anything close to it—not apes, not elephants, not dolphins, not bees, not butterflies.

Money differs from what we might expect in that it is not really *owned* by anyone, although it is *used* by almost everyone. In fact, if we owned the money we use, we might not find it quite so universally accepted. If money were owned, people who do not like us might not accept our bills in payment. If all of Bill Gates' wealth had his name engraved on each note he spent, his rivals might gang together and refuse to take that money in an effort to do him in.

Money is a collective idea—like the English language, the days of the week, or the latest joke—that people employ, contribute to, pass around, and adhere to, but do not actually own individually. Martha Stewart, for example, may create meals, floral arrangements, and other decorations used in the celebrations of Thanksgiving, Christmas, Hanukkah, and Kwanzaa, but she doesn't own those holidays. She *uses* them and so do we. They are collective notions, things we hold in common culturally and abide by, like the speed limit and other aspects of the law.

I learned the hard way that we do not own our money. When I was six years old I went with my mother to a nearby bank to open my first account. I deposited into that account two new $20 bills my grandfather had given me. A few months later, I went back to the bank to take out that money. But instead of *my* two $20 bills, the teller handed me three $10 bills and two $5 bills. When I told her that she had made a big mistake—that I had given her two new $20 bills—she laughed and explained that the bank had given my money to someone else, but that the money she now gave me was in every way equal to what I had put in. She said the three $10s and two $5s I was holding were just as good as *my* two $20s.

Needless to say, it took me a very long time to trust that bank again, but when I did it was because I must have come to the realization that you never own your money. What you own is the *amount* of money you control or are allowed to use. That amount is determined by lots of things in addition to luck. It depends on what you do for a living, how well you are paid, and how well your investments are doing. By extension, it also applies to how much you can borrow, which is a function of the items listed previously and how promptly you repaid what you were previously lent.

Money is one of those things whose *reality* increases the more people believe in it and use it. Since nearly everyone in the world believes in the dollar, you can buy, sell, and price almost anything with it—licit and illicit. Oil, gold, coal, and airfares are priced in dollars. So are blood transfusions, Ferraris, and crack cocaine. Saints and sinners may not agree on many things, but they agree on the utility of a dollar. They also agree that although a stack of $20s may have just been used to pay for something dastardly or even deadly, the bills themselves should not be considered tainted by the nefarious business dealings of their users. Who really cares what the money on the church collection plate was doing the night before?

A NEW TYPE OF MONEY

My great-grandfather thought he knew what money really was; so did my Soviet-era friends. To them, money was something you could trade for goods and services, which meant that it had some sort of intrinsic value. In their eyes, money was something *official*. It had to be *issued* by a mint (not just printed or stamped!), it had to be decorated with government seals, crests, invocations, prayers, dead politicians' profiles, and obscure figures from Greek mythology. It had to be transported under guard and treated with respect. For them, money had to look like, well, *money*, which meant it had to be instantly recognizable. For them, money needed backing, which meant that each coin or note had to have a government-mandated link to a unit of gold or silver, a point we will come back to later.

Economists agree with most of the above, but also argue that money must be more. Usually, they say money must have at least three well-defined qualities: It must be a store of value, a medium of exchange, and a unit of account. By *store of value*, they mean it has to hold its purchasing power even if it is forgotten under a sofa cushion for a couple of years.

By *medium of exchange*, they mean other people must be willing to accept it to settle debts or pay for goods, irrespective of who gives it to them.

And by *unit of account*, they mean each unit has to have a discrete mathematical value that can be added, multiplied, or divided so that goods can be priced and other things, like profits and losses, can be figured out. Money's value has to be measurable.

Money, in some form (cash, check, or electronic deposits) symbolizes that we are in possession of a certain measurable quantity of purchasing power. Purchasing power is the bedrock assumption that makes money work. Because it is so abstract, it is completely convertible. As a result, if two people combine their households, the value of a week's worth of work at the automobile factory can be added without incident to the value of a week's worth of work by the dental chair. The combined purchasing power of those salaries—dentist and auto worker—can be used to buy shares of stock, vacation homes, lottery tickets, or the products of a farm or ranch, without any difficulty whatsoever.

This is not a point that should be glossed over. Money as a symbol of purchasing power has real might and real magic.

Money's might lies in the fact that it conveys buying power from one person to another—no matter what they do—in a form that has efficacy and convenience. To allow money to do that requires a belief in it and in the people who manage it.

Money's magic lies in the fact that it can transmit buying power over time. A significant number of people are living very well today because they inherited some measure of buying power from family members who died years, even generations, ago. Many of those people are investing that money in projects that will pay off in the future. They are taking buying power that was accumulated in the railroad-building era and investing it in newly formed companies in the biotech era.

For the majority of human history—the 100,000 years or so when we made our living hunting and gathering—it would have been unthinkable to hand down buying power.

We could hand down a few keepsakes of some value—objects we made or found—but we could not store their worth.

MONEY AS *BELIEF*

In a certain way, money requires a kind of group hypnosis. That's how the buy-in works at first. From the moment a young child is told—*and then believes*—that there is more buying power locked inside the little dime than the big nickel (or that a $1 bill is worth less than a $20 bill), she is hooked. The idea that buying power can be symbolized is conveyed to her. A belief in money, of course, says nothing about equity and whether the men and women who twist bolts onto truck wheels should receive less than the men and women in the executive suite. In fact, money is disinterested, a kind of economic ambergris, a substance completely without odor once used by perfume makers to trap and hold their most delightful scents.

Money is not only a method for exchanging buying power from one person to another, it also allows the exchange of buying power between people of different cultures and countries, within limits.

Among the big-time currencies of the world (dollars, pounds, yen, euros, as well as a few others) exchangeability is nearly instant and universal, though the exact ratio of one currency to another shifts frequently depending upon a host of things, including differences in interest rates between countries, demand for products and services, and sentiment.

As a result, I can go to an automated teller machine in nearly any of the countries issuing the above-listed currencies and within seconds withdraw from my American bank a sum of dollars that is instantly converted into the currency of wherever I am. I can put in my card, tap in my PIN number, and out will come euros, yen, pounds, or whatever.

And yet, some currencies—and some countries—are not in the loop. I cannot go to an ATM in Burundi or Chad or Peru or Cuba and withdraw local currencies from my American bank account. I cannot withdraw local currencies *everywhere* because in addition to being a symbol, money is also a *system*. Like all systems, the money system requires membership, which in turn requires an adherence to a uniform set of rules as well as access to an institutional and technological infrastructure. But more about that later.

HOW MONEY IS CREATED

So where exactly does money come from?

The nation's money supply is like a set of barbershop mirrors into which you can look and see yourself reflected an infinite number of times while your beard is being trimmed or your hair is being cut. It grows each time it is lent. The money supply exists, for the most part, as a result of banks. Let me explain what I mean.

The way money creation works, in a simplified manner, is that after a person is paid $100 for performing a service or selling a good, he deposits that money into his bank.

The bank lists on the depositor's account that he owns or, more appropriately, has use of $100. Because banking regulators always get into the act, they tell the banks to reserve, let's say, 10 percent of all they take on deposit in case of emergencies. As a result, when the depositor leaves the bank, the loan officer can lend out $90 of the original $100 deposit to someone else, who then puts it in her bank, which now says she has use of $90. The first bank lists a deposit of $100, the second a deposit of $90, for a total of $190, nearly double the original amount.

At the second bank, 90 percent of the $90 can be lent out again. That means someone else can take that money and deposit it into an account and by so doing have access to $81 of bank funds.

At this bank, 90 percent of the newly deposited $81 can be lent out again to someone else who then deposits 90 percent of that—$72.90—into his account.

Ninety percent of $72.90 is $65.61, which can now be lent and deposited in another bank, which means that if the initial $100 were deposited and lent out throughout the banking system, over time it would expand into about $1000, if 10 percent were held in reserve at each banking institution.

Of course when you deposit money, you receive interest from your bank and when you borrow, the bank requires interest of you. As a result, higher interest rates slow down the pace of lending (and the growth of the money "supply") while lower rates make monetary growth happen faster.

The bottom line is that the amount of money available to spend expands as the nation's overall level of debt grows. Bank-created money is actually a form of debt, which is one reason why banks call their deposits *liabilities*—because they want to lend them—and their loans *assets,* something they always want more of.

But where does the initial $100 come from?

That's the *really* interesting part.

Money comes into existence when the Federal Reserve, the nation's central bank and its primary banking regulator, simply decides to print some more. When it does, it issues nicely designed, nicely printed notes that say they are promises to pay the bearer upon demand the sum listed on the face of the bill. Government money is really just an IOU.

Excuse me?

That's right. A dollar is simply the government's promise to pay you, well, a dollar. That's all it is.

Money is not backed by gold, silver, red hot chile peppers, sawdust, or rabbit ears. It is not backed by anything tangible. As a consequence, it is—in a way—a circular argument. ("I, the government, promise to pay you, the bearer, a dollar if you, the bearer, are already holding a dollar in your hand."). The power of money is that if you bring a dollar to any bank in the country, that bank, acting on behalf of the government, will give you a dollar in exchange. That is all the bank will do in order to guarantee the value of the nation's currency. (The only other thing they will do is attempt to stop you if you try to steal money that is not under your control or if you try to deface or destroy bills or coins.)

Money is a set of barbershop mirrors, but it was not always this way.

OLD-TIME MONEY

In the good old days, before August 15, 1971, when President Nixon unilaterally uncoupled the dollar from its longstanding link to gold, a dollar had a government-mandated value. That value was measured in standardized weights of gold (and before that in silver and gold). In those days, when the Soviet Union was at its overly muscled height and the Vietnam War was raging, Nixon said the value of a dollar would no longer be equal to $\frac{1}{35}$ of an ounce of gold. Hitherto, its value was to be fixed by the market. Dollars would become direct symbols for units of buying power, not stand-ins for gold, which in turn was a stand-in for buying power. Dollars—and their attendant buying power—would be worth as much as the market said they were worth. And markets value things, like stocks, bonds, and dollars, at least in part, as a result of sentiment.

More than two decades after the fact, when I was writing about money, the economic jury was still out as to whether currencies without a link to a commodity like gold or silver could survive for very long. People wondered, What was the yardstick of value? How could a dollar keep its buying power intact when it was really only *exchangeable* for itself?

At the time, I was dubious about such an abstract fellow as the unbaked dollar. I felt that the dollar needed to be tied to something real. It did not have to be a precious metal like gold or silver; it could have been a basket of wheat, a bale of hay, or a ton of steel.

My view was that money needed a link to something with a finite quantity, like gold, to serve as a brake and slow down its creation. If each dollar needed $\frac{1}{35}$ of an ounce of gold to back it up before it could come into creation, the number of dollars in circulation would be limited to the amount of gold that could be dug out of the ground. That would make money creation a slower process, so the ocean of liquidity would expand less rapidly and prices would rise at an orderly and sustainable pace. Rather than simply commanding the printing presses to roll, the Federal Reserve would have to determine first whether there was sufficient gold in reserve to keep the dollar's buying power fixed at one dollar–to–$\frac{1}{35}$ of an ounce. If there was insufficient gold, it would have to put a brake on the expansion of the money supply by raising interest rates.

I held that view because in the decades after Nixon uncoupled the dollar from gold, the entire world experienced a tremendous bout of inflation. Prices for nearly everything soared. Within a relatively short period of time, oil rose from $4 to $40 a barrel, gold went from $35 an ounce to more than $800 an ounce, silver rose from $4 an ounce to $40 an ounce, while housing prices increased ten-fold. The only way for the Federal Reserve to stop these runaway prices from rising further was to raise interest rates as high as 18 percent, which slowed the economy to a halt. At 18 percent, borrowing stopped, recession was upon us, prices for everything began to fall.

Jamming on the emergency brake to stop inflation always seemed to me like a poor way to run the world's primary economic engine, the United States. In the post–World War II period, up to the mid-1970s, growth was orderly, inflation was in check, and interest rates were low. During that era, Europe and Japan recovered in the aftermath of World War II and billions of people in Europe and the developing world were lifted out of abject poverty and into the middle class.

The stable, dollar-into-gold system seemed to work pretty well until the Vietnam War, when the U.S. government printed money to pay for the fighting without regard to how much gold it had in its vaults. Back then, in the late '60s and early '70s, America had hundreds of billions of dollars in circulation in the United States and abroad (all foreign dollar holdings were immediately convertible into gold upon demand) but only about $14 billion in bullion on deposit in the Fort Knox vaults. The printing presses had been rolling to pay for the war but the steam shovels had fallen silent. Something was clearly out of whack. President Nixon, faced with a slumping economy, demanded that Europeans turn their overseas dollars into gold, and the need for even more funds to pay for the war separated the dollar from gold. With the stroke of a pen, the post–World War II system was brought to an end.

REGULATING PRICES

And then the Zen (or perhaps Seinfeld) logic of it all dawned on me. When a currency is backed by *nothing* (the government's promise might as well be the grin on the Cheshire Cat in *Alice's Adventures in Wonderland*), it is really backed by *everything*. What I mean by that is that the overall supply of money   the amount of it in circulation is what determines all prices. And yet, if the number of nifty new things constantly increases—new Game Boys, new electric power plants, new homes, new stocks and bonds—then the dollars in circulation will have somewhere to go besides raising prices, as long as the overall level of interest rates is low enough to make buying these items easy to do. Make more products (and sell what you make) and then everyone who wants to work can find a job.

In addition, if the gates to the country are open, and foreign goods are allowed in, then domestic producers will be forced to keep their prices low, another antidote to inflation. Competition from Europe's Airbus keeps

Boeing's prices reasonable; competition from Japan's Toyota keeps GM's prices from rising too high.

Inflation due to too much money chasing too few goods (or too much money chasing just enough goods) could be curtailed if the number of goods and services in circulation (the ones that people really like) expands as well. Growth is the cure-all to an expanding money supply.

But there is a trick to managing the growth option correctly. To do it right, the Fed has to allow the money supply to increase at a rate that is just slightly ahead of economic growth. As a result, the Fed can print more money without inflation if it does so only when there are more S.U.V.s (foreign or domestic), restaurant meals, PCs, and cell phones to buy. Just as the limiting factor to non-inflationary growth in the old world of gold was the rate at which the yellow metal could be dug out of the ground, the limiting factor in the world of unbacked dollars is the growth of the economy itself. Match the money supply to the country's overall rate of growth (and keep competition robust) and inflation will be kept at bay.

Under Alan Greenspan, chairman of the Federal Reserve, the nation's money supply and growth rates have tracked nicely. The only hiccups in the system came in 1990, when the Fed slowed the growth of the money supply, when it feared it had put too much money into circulation in the wake of the 1987 crash and its aftermath, and in 1999 and 2000, when the Fed at first increased the money supply to protect the economy from a possible jolt due to the turning of the millennium (the Y2K bug), and then tightened the money supply in early 2000, after the Y2K bug failed to materialize. In both instances economic slowdowns followed within half a year or so of the Fed applying the brakes. Aside from these two bumps,

Alan Greenspan's stewardship of the Fed has been masterful.

There is another element in the mix that helps keep inflation at bay: the financial markets.

If money stores buying power, and too much of it is around, it will drive up the price of real-world things like coffee, tea, eyeglasses, and insurance, unless the supply of those things expands. But if people view the markets as safe and well regulated—and they have confidence in the future—then people will store a good measure of that buying power in the financial markets. In addition to buying dishwashers, people will buy stock in dishwasher manufacturers, which is why the markets have grown so much over the last decade.

If dollars are like batteries charged with units of buying power, the financial markets (stocks and bonds) are like power lines that put such buying power to use. They do so by giving money to companies to enable them to grow. And, of course, the more money that rolls into the markets, the higher its price level. But while higher prices for goods and services are bad, higher market prices are good for three big reasons.

First, by giving companies more money with which to invest, stock and bond purchasers are helping companies make the wheels of the economy turn faster. Investment capital means new plants and more mergers aimed at creating efficiencies. Ultimately, this type of investment leads to higher levels of employment.

Second, higher prices for stocks means that companies obtain capital less expensively. They do so because the price for investment capital is a share of the profits a company makes. Companies return a percentage of their profits to their shareholders based on the number of shares that are outstanding. If those shares sell for $10, and the company has profits equal to $1 a share, then the price per share that it pays for that capital is 10 percent. But if the share price rises to $100, and the profits remain the same, then the price per share for access to that capital falls to only 1 percent. Higher share prices make life a lot easier for companies.

The third reason why rising stock prices are good—at least in my opinion—is that they make people feel *rich*. Not only do growing markets shift money from consumers to producers so the economy as a whole is built up bigger, they also make people feel better as they watch their net worth grow. As a result, doctors and lawyers—not to mention engineers and mechanics—seeing their wealth accumulate in the stock market are less inclined to raise their fees and are more likely to spend money. The so-called wealth effect keeps spending levels high and prices stable.

For these and other reasons, the growth of the capital markets has proven to be an unexpected but powerful escape valve for inflation.

Even though money is a circular promise, the Federal Reserve and the world's other central bankers still have a powerful tool for regulating the size of the supply. By making that supply larger—or by draining the ocean of funds—the Fed can influence the overall price level and with it can influence the level and rate of economic activity.

It can do this by offering for sale billions of dollars worth of Treasury bonds and notes with higher than current-level interest rates.

As investors rush to buy those bonds, they take money out of their banks, out of the stock market, and out of circulation. When depositors take money out of their banks, the banks have less money to lend and in many cases have to either borrow money from other banks or call in their outstanding loans. When banks borrow from each other, they do so at a rate called the Fed Funds rate, which the Federal Reserve controls. When that rate is steep, borrowing is curtailed and banks are forced to call in their outstanding loans.

By calling in outstanding loans, the barbershop mirror of money creation works in reverse and money disappears, out of sight. Rather than having a deposit of $100 grow into $1000 through bank lending, the Fed (in theory) can force banks to shrink that $1000 all the way down to its original $100 deposit. The Fed also controls the amount of money banks must keep in reserve—a very big level and one that it rarely uses.

To spur the economy, when prices are falling because money is in short supply, the Federal Reserve (via the Treasury) has the authority to call in (buy back) its outstanding bonds. When it buys back its bonds, it does it by printing dollars. The effect of this action is to put more money into circulation.

EXCHANGE RATES

The world's central bankers have become highly adept at managing the world's system of money. They have kept inflation low and have kept sufficient money in circulation to prod growth. The big countries have been able to maintain confidence in their currencies for the most part. But what really determines the value of one currency against another? The short answer is market perceptions and sentiment.

Each day more than $1 trillion in currencies are traded on the world's money exchanges. Most of that money is privately held and speculative. Because a few big currencies are used for most of the world's financial transactions—dollars, pounds, yen, and euros—they are constantly being exchanged for one another. Smaller currencies—Israeli shekels, for example—are traded when countries settle up their trade accounts. Small countries like to keep large amounts of dollars around so they do not have to buy or sell their own currencies all the time. Everyone takes dollars, but not everyone takes shekels. And yet, if you want to purchase something made or grown in Israel, you need to convert your currency into shekels to do it. Currency transactions that are used to settle trade transactions are in the minority.

Most trade in currencies is defensive. An American company buys euros today to protect against the value of the dollar falling against euros tomorrow. This is speculation since the company could guess incorrectly. If it does, the "hedge" against currency shifts would result in losses. As a result, most companies buy multiple currencies as hedges—or retain brokers to do it for them—to prevent losses due to the value of the dollar rising or falling.

The purchase or sale of currencies to prevent future losses is speculation and it is why most currency trading occurs. The market takes a view about America's prospects for the future with regard to growth, interest rates, and confidence and it translates that view of the future into a price for the dollar. When people believe strongly in America, the dollar is strong. When they see America founder, with growth faltering (and lower interest rates on their way to remedy slowing growth) the dollar tends to weaken.

So what determines the value of the dollar or any other currency?

It is the way in which the issuing country and its prospects for the future are viewed. Since no one knows this for certain, collective sentiment is what makes America's circular argument worth what it is worth vis-à-vis the circular arguments of Britain, the European Union, or Japan.

A nation's currency may no longer be a proxy for gold, but it is a proxy for the way that nation's prospects are collectively viewed by the market.

In other words, the one item you can never remove from the barbershop mirror is the head of the person getting the shave. It—and its views—are magnified forever.

CHAPTER FOUR

What Markets Need in Order to Work

Fast-forward from the baggy-suited Soviets of yesteryear to today's svelte Russians. Things still do not work quite right in the land of gulags and caviar, but progress is being made and a new elite is emerging. The wholesale demolition of the creaky Soviet-era system is now more or less complete. Commissars and high-ranking KGB officers in Stalin-era Zil limousines have been replaced by businessmen, gangsters, and foreign investors in bullet-proof Mercedeses with reinforced tires. The favor bank of communism, in which one bureaucrat would get his way by doing a favor for another, has been replaced by an economy in which few things get done without a bribe, often concealed as a commission or business expense. As a result, state *secrecy* has been replaced by business *opacity*. A true market economy—with capital unfettered, available, and priced at the going international rate—still remains a goal. What the Russians need now to make the magic of the market work for them is what economists call institution building. They are partway there.

So why bring this up? This is a book about how markets work, after all, not how to get Russia back on its feet.

I do so to illustrate that capital and the *money* economy are not things; they are systems that deftly balance the human and the material to yield prices, among other things, along with prosperity, if they are managed correctly. Market-driven prices are the bedrock proposition of the market economy, which, since the end of World War II, has helped lift billions of people out of poverty. It is a wondrous thing, a magnificent creation of the mind that enables people to turn their dreams (not to mention their nightmares) into reality. It works, according to Joseph Schumpeter, a gifted economist of the twentieth century, like a self-cleaning oven. When capitalism splatters out of control, with companies and institutions failing, you simply turn up the heat of growth and incinerate all the mess. Economic growth is the boon of the market system and its secret weapon. Until the market economy was invented, stasis and stagnation were the rules. Economic growth is something new in human history. Along with growth comes prosperity.

If well-trained, well-educated people combine capital with accurately arrived-at prices and have set up a functioning money system, they can move mountains, finance freeways, and build dream houses with cool blue David Hockney–style swimming pools. For this reason, capital, because of everything it enables people to do, is a very powerful force. The old communists did not understand this fact. They valued the hammer and the sickle, but not the bank or the mutual fund. They trained hundreds of thousands of scientists, engineers, technicians, and industrial workers, but no stock pickers, money managers, or financial specialists. Although they funded massive development projects, like the Kama River truck-manufacturing plant, the world's largest at the time, they considered profits evil and shareholders as freeloaders. As a consequence, there was no way to impose what economists call *market efficiencies* on the old Soviet system. Rather than having a group of angry shareholders vote out of office an incompetent CEO because he was not efficient enough to do quality work and return a profit, the Soviets had only Siberia.

Capital, according to Hernando de Soto, a Peruvian economist, social activist, and philosopher, is a "mystery." It is a mystery because of its ability to transform the planet and the way we allocate everything we produce and consume. It is a mystery because of its ability to help organize our efforts. And it is a mystery because of the way in which it enables people to change the way they think about value.

Allow me to explain what I mean.

In Peru (or much of Russia, India, China, Africa, or South America, for that matter), a house is merely a dwelling place. If you visit Lima, you will see a massive, *unreal city* (with apologies to T.S. Eliot) of slums, hovels, and houses on the outskirts of the *real* capital city of Peru. As many as three million Peruvians live in this jumble of homes that, for the most part, does not exist according to the local authorities, due to the fact that these homes— even offices and factories—were built largely by squatters or by people with what we might call "dubious" claims on the land. (Similar "unreal" cities exist on the outskirts of Bombay, Calcutta, Caracas, Mexico City, São Paulo, Manila—the list goes on with hundreds of millions of people living in dwelling places that are a legal never-never land.)

In these unreal areas the streets have no officially recognized names, the buildings have no officially recognized addresses, and the people have no inviolate claims on their houses. In fact, in many areas of the world the right of a home owner to his property is pretty poorly defined and there is scant legal protection. In China, for example, homes were demolished without compensation to make way for the Olympics. In Israel, suspected terrorists can have their home bulldozed into the ground. In much of the world, a family's home is not its castle—protected by law—but the government's plaything.

Because home owners in many countries are not protected by the rules, processes, and procedures of the world's capital-oriented legal systems, development lags. People can live in their homes, but because there are no legal protections those homes are merely dwelling places, not *assets* to be tapped.

This is significant. Solve the mystery of capital and you solve many seemingly intractable problems along with it, so says de Soto. If, for example, governments protected and defended legal titles (ironclad ownership rights) in a manner similar to the way they are defended in the United States and other advanced countries, then a family dwelling place would become a capital asset. When that transformation occurs, the family can borrow money against its home. When ownership is sacrosanct, the magic of the market goes to work. If a home cannot be bulldozed without a court order and compensation—and cannot be seized or given to someone else without legal due process—then that home has *value* that can be quantified and employed.

Don't get me wrong. Clear title to a hovel located along an unnamed street will not suddenly transform the hovel into a Beverly Hills mansion. But the fact that that hovel is owned will convey to its owners many more degrees of freedom. The first freedom is that no one can demolish your home without legal action and compensation. The second freedom is that if you occupy a home that cannot be demolished, no one can build on top of you, which means that land becomes scarce. The third freedom is that scarcity increases value, which is why cartels form to limit the production of oil or the number of diamonds in circulation.

If the amount of value in a home is measurable, the owner can go to a bank or a lending cooperative and borrow against it. Perhaps the family cannot borrow much money, but if its members can borrow enough to buy a sewing machine and a set of carpenter's tools, then they have found a pathway to self-sufficiency. On a grander scale, in the United States, where homes have substantial value, a great many executives, entrepreneurial juices flowing, have borrowed against their homes to start thriving businesses. EDS, a computer firm now worth many billions of dollars, began as a second mortgage on Ross Perot's house.

There is another aspect to the magic of capital. By transforming *things* into assets, through the power of ownership, capital imposes discipline.

In the unreal city, life may be rough-and-tumble, but dwelling places are free. Obtain some materials, legally or illegally, hammer them together, and you have a home.

But in the world of capital, things are different. You cannot simply build a home. First, you must obtain title to the land. To do that you probably have to borrow money or tap into your savings. Either way, you have to be forward looking and capable of earning a living in order to obtain your plot of land, which means you must be productive. In addition, if you default on your loan, you lose your ownership claim. As a result, entrepreneurs borrowing against their homes to become tailors or carpenters (or Silicon Valley entrepreneurs) do so knowing that failure could be accompanied by a severe penalty, the loss of a home. A threat like that tends to focus the mind.

MARKETS ARE NOT SUFFICIENT

In order to work, the world's money system requires markets. In addition, it requires institutional infrastructure, such as government-owned or -controlled central banks; privately held merchant, investment, and commercial banks; stock exchanges; and bond markets. These are the bricks and beams Russia is using (and which the United States used previously) to build the institutional component of its economy. And while it may seem simple, institution building is really quite an intricate job. No wonder that there have been missteps. No wonder that when the first wave of privatization occurred in Russia, and the government sold off or gave away companies, a few "oligarchs" absconded with so many of the biggest prizes. TV stations, newspapers, Aeroflot, container ships, and docking rights, for example, went to a few politically connected individuals. Russia's emerging political and legal systems could not keep pace. In fact, there was privatization before there were laws that clearly defined private property.

Creating a market economy takes time and is given to trial and error. In addition, it has to be accomplished in "real time," meaning that you cannot stop flying Aeroflot's airplanes or producing Gazprom's natural gas and oil as you cobble together a market economy. Capitalism happens at the speed of the trading floor, which is to say, at the speed of the world's computers, but politics moves at the speed of a good argument. Once a *market* event happens, it takes a long time for the government to catch up.

To illustrate that point, in the United States the market meltdown of October 19, 1987, took fewer than four hours to reap its deadly blow on the nation's collective wallet. When it was over, a few weeks later, Congress voted to look into the cause of the problem. It constituted a blue-ribbon commission that sought testimony from brokers, traders, economists, market participants, and academics. Nine months later, the commission issued its report on what happened and suggested ways to prevent another meltdown. A few of the commission's recommendations—to stop trading in individual stocks or in the market as a whole if a plunge were to occur—were put into effect, with mixed results.

This is not an apology for bad behavior or government tardiness. It is simply an effort to show that the magic of the market is complicated and that it takes time to construct. In the United States and in many other countries, the financial infrastructure of banks and markets has been in existence for decades if not centuries. In addition, the physical infrastructure of computers and communications systems has been developing for decades.

This complicated physical infrastructure of the markets can clear billions of checks each night and move money electronically among millions of checking accounts located inside thousands of competing banks. The system, which in the United States is supervised by the Fed, has its own communications system and protocols and enables banks to tally up their credits and debits with security and privacy. The system represents an overall investment of hundreds of billions of dollars. It did not happen overnight.

THE MARKETS ARE MADE UP OF COMMUNITIES

But while the physical and technological infrastructures are necessary, they are not sufficient. The world of money also requires dozens of "specialist" communities that in the aggregate constitute the larger global financial community.

These specialist communities—which are abundant in the United States and in a number of advanced market-economy countries—have yet to fully emerge in Russia and in most developing nations.

Who makes up these communities? They are made up of tens of thousands of bank credit analysts as well as stockbrokers and bankers of all stripes. They are also made up of technicians who build, program, and maintain the many millions of computers that are the foundation of the money system. And they are made up of tens of thousands of stock analysts, bond analysts, fund managers, and salespeople. The communities contain thousands of people who manage bank and insurance risk and consult and advise managers on ways to select stocks and balance portfolios.

Behind these are other communities of capitalism—accountants and lawyers as well as the thousands of people who work in the government's supervisory and oversight bodies, like the Securities and Exchange Commission as well as the Fed. And there are financial and market economists as well as forecasters.

To keep these communities functioning at world-class levels, the infrastructure of the markets includes teachers and trainers as well as professors at colleges, universities, and business schools. These people work with publishers to develop, organize, edit, and produce business, financial, legal, and accounting information.

On top of these communities (or at the bottom, depending upon your view) there are print, TV, radio, newsletter, and on-line journalists who follow the markets, draw attention to what investors are doing, create and disseminate the *buzz,* and occasionally push a thumb or two in the eyes of people with power.

Have I left out anybody? Probably.

A smoothly functioning market economy depends upon it being populated with people in each of these communities. In an economy as large as the United States, it takes millions of well-trained, well-educated people to make up the communities that make up the financial world—from the people who install the ATMs to those who interview bond traders on CNN. It costs trillions of dollars to educate, train, and organize the communities that regulate and populate the markets.

At present, in most of the world, these communities are sadly lacking, or they are new and without much experience. In 1990, a professor from Harvard could have hopped on a plane, flown to the Soviet Union, and handed then-President Gorbachev a "to do" list for creating a market economy. But the real work of creating an economy is far more difficult and far more complex, and it cannot be created overnight or on the cheap. In the United States, Britain, and in much of Europe, it has taken hundreds of years of trial and error to create today's market economy and to train people to do all the necessary jobs. In Japan they have been at it for *only* 150 years—and it shows.

THE POWER OF OWNERSHIP

One of the higher truths laid out so far in this chapter is that the system of money which we have created is based upon a set of concepts that enables people to capture and store *buying power* in the things we own. The amount of buying power we accrue in the purchase of an asset such as a house can actually grow if we maintain the home and are lucky enough to have purchased it in an area that retains its allure. Stocks, bonds, options, futures contracts are all derived from the concept that an owner's rights are inviolate.

The system of money in existence in the developed world functions because ownership is seldom in doubt and when it is in doubt, the money system has powerful mechanisms like courts and arbitration panels to resolve any questions. In fact, ownership is such a big deal that in many instances it is a crime to conceal who actually owns what, like a stock or a bank account. Because ownership is so well developed, rights can be attached to it. For example, shareholders generally have a right to vote on (or veto) proposals made by management with regard to takeovers, board seats, and auditing firms.

There is another item to consider regarding ownership and the global money system. Generally, we think of
assets as things—gold, diamonds, homes, ships, land. For
much of human history, only a few narrowly defined
classes of people were allowed to own assets like these. In
fact, for much of human history, people themselves were
owned either as slaves or as people who pledged their loy-
alty to their leaders. People who were allowed to own such
assets could do with them as they pleased.

More recently, shares of companies were added to the
list of assets. Congealed in a stock certificate is an ownership stake in a company as well as a claim to a share of
the company's profits, should the directors and management deign to give you some. Along with most shares go
voting rights. Because the money system has a strong bias
toward ownership and believes it is important, you can
buy and sell shares after they have been issued, which is
one of the purposes of stock markets. And, because the
rights of a shareholder are contained within the stock
rather than granted to an individual, anybody—good or
bad, tall or short—can exercise those rights once they own
the stock. The rules and infrastructure of the market economy make that possible.

That is an important point. In politics, the rights of
citizenship go to the citizen. In the realm of markets,
rights go with whoever owns the stock or bond. Because
stocks, bonds, and other related products contain ownership rights, owners can divide and subdivide these products to form other products. From that standpoint, you can
buy a stock or bond or the constituent products that make
them up. You can cut stocks and bonds into pieces or take
other items and form them into financial vehicles.

Let's begin with bonds, which are also called securities. In their essence, bonds are really loans to companies or governments or even individuals. Generally they have a principal amount and a stream of interest the borrowing entity must pay. Because rights are the property of the bond holder, some bright investors have been able to buy dozens of corporate bonds, bundle them together, and sell the interest income to one set of investors and the repayment of the principal to others. Because these income streams are sold at a slight discount, the packager makes money doing this.

In addition, some financial managers create their own securities or "bonds." They do so by gathering into packages dozens of the same type of loans. Car loans, home mortgages, and aircraft loans are commonly "securitized" this way. By doing so, mortgage-initiating banks have an outlet where they can sell their mortgages, allowing them to make a profit for having issued the loan. Your home mortgage made by a local bank may have been bundled up and sold with dozens of other mortgages to an investment fund or a pension fund.

The same is true for car loans. Ford or GM, for example, can put together a $10-million package of identical car loans with identical terms and sell them to investors like insurance companies.

In both instances a real asset—a home or a car—makes the investment less risky for the buyer of the loan. In each instance, risk is further reduced because investors are purchasing dozens—even hundreds—of loans in a single package. While a single car buyer or home owner in the package may have fallen on hard times, chances are the overall group of borrowers is in pretty good shape. In fact, packagers and investors have sophisticated math programs that can calculate the risk and price the package accordingly.

Conducting these types of activities on a routine basis is the business of the millions of people who make up the sophisticated communities of finance. They make money available for average citizens to buy houses and cars. And, by making that money available, they turn those houses and cars into investment assets for another group of people.

You can imagine the market economy working this way. An employee at a car company borrows money to buy a car. By doing so, he helps keep himself and his colleagues employed building automobiles. That fellow's car loan is bundled up and sold to a pension fund in which he has invested a portion of his 401(k). Because he is employed, has a partially paid-off car, and has money in his pension plan, he can find a house, go to a bank, and take out a mortgage. The bank then sells the mortgage to a packager, who sells it to a mutual fund in which the automobile worker and his neighbors have some of their money invested. Because the auto worker has a car, a house, a pension, and some investments, he can apply for credit cards from his bank and from individual stores. (These credit card issues also sell their outstanding loans, called receivables, to investors like mutual funds and pension plans.) As a result, the *system* of money has many ways in which it supports itself and fosters growth while at the same time spreading the risk among many investors. By granting buying power to individuals by issuing credit—while spreading the risk of bad loans among countless investors—the system feeds on itself and fosters growth in an ingenious manner with a high level of safety.

Stocks—also called equities—are claims on future earnings as well as ownership stakes, as I've already noted. Stock owners can sell the right to someone else to buy the stocks they own at a future time at a price agreed upon today. By doing so, they provide money to companies and to the market, but limit their own risk by locking in a sale at a future price.

Options are one type of right that stock investors can sell. There are even markets where options can be traded. An investor owning shares can sell an option for $.50, to buy a share of his stock at a future date for $10. If the buyer of that option watches the stock soar to $20, he will make a hefty profit on his $.50 investment because he can exercise his option to buy the stock for $10 while simultaneously selling it for $20. However, if the stock falls to $8 a share, rather than lose $2 a share, which he would have done had he owned the stock, the option buyer simply lets his option lapse, having lost only $.50. For the seller of the option, rather than losing $2 a share when the stock drops to $8, he only loses $1.50, because he can pocket the $.50 he made selling the option.

Trading options is not without risk, however. Consider that the oldest bank in Britain, Barings Bank, was brought down by a so-called rogue trader using options. From his base in Singapore, Nick Leeson, the trader, bought put and call options on the Nikkei, Japan's stock market. (*Call* options are those in which the seller of the option gives the buyer the right to buy shares at a set price for a given period of time. A *put* option is one that gives its buyer the right to sell the underlying stock at a predetermined price. The seller of the put option is obligated to buy the stock at the predetermined price.) By buying both puts and calls, Leeson was hoping to minimize his risk. If the market went moderately up or moderately down, he was covered. But what the young trader did not foresee was that Japan would be hit by a massive earthquake in Kobe just after he bought the options. The quake caused the Nikkei to plummet. Leeson's strategy of covering his downside risk while maximizing his upside potential using options failed. When it was over, Leeson lost more than $1 billion of the bank's money. The British government rushed in and Barings was sold to a Dutch financial firm called ING.

There are other strategies for limiting risk that we will go into later. However, the point of all this is that the markets are really wonderful ways to make capital available and to do so in ways that minimize risk.

Markets are complicated mechanisms that cannot be created overnight. The bedrock proposition upon which they rest is that ownership is sacred. Having the right to own something gives a person the right to divide and subdivide it. Each time a piece that is divided or subdivided can be sold, or "optioned," to someone else, the risks associated with ownership decline.

The elegance of markets is contained within the fact that, while they are adept at getting capital to people who need it—entrepreneurs, home owners, car buyers, credit card users—they are equally adept at making certain that if an individual or even a sector of the economy suffers, the entire system will not go down.

CHAPTER FIVE

How to Think About Stocks

WHO SAYS IT IS A RATIONAL MARKET?

Markets are structures that require communities of people to run them. Those who do so are not necessarily altruists. They are there for the money. Profits from investment—as well as the joy of continually solving investment and economic puzzles—draw people to work on Wall Street and its environs. Without profits, the corridors of the Street would be silent and Manhattan—for all its foibles and greatness—would still be an important city, but not the world's capital of capitalism.

So let me begin this chapter by contradicting myself—not entirely, I won't give you that, but just a bit. A lot of people have made a lot of money over the years in the markets for individual stocks, bonds, and other products, despite factors like sentiment. The fact that people make money in the world of finance is what keeps its wheels turning and its computers humming. Without an ample supply of filthy lucre, the affluent suburbs of New York would still be grazing land.

Investors have made money despite the market's overall direction at any point in time and advice from the pundits. They have done it legitimately, thoughtfully, and repeatedly. And, they have done it despite the fact that more than one theory in economics suggests that making money buying and selling individual stocks over the long haul is next to impossible.

To be sure, making money picking stocks is not easy. The theories say that it is difficult because prediction is impossible. These theories say that stock pickers win only by following the momentum of the market. The reason for their pessimism is that each share of a company moves in a more or less independent fashion, jostled by the economy, the company's performance, the performance of each of the economy's *sectors* (software, high-tech, financial services, automotive, and so on). As a result, the theory suggests, news reports, the prospects of a region of the country or the world where the company is weak or strong, along with many other intangibles, determine price in a manner that mere mortals cannot fathom for very long. Yes, we can all be lucky. Yes, we can make money over the short term. But over the long haul, we are probably better off throwing darts at a list of stocks and buying the ones where the darts land than we are intuiting an individual stock's performance over the next eighteen months.

With so many factors determining price, believers in what is called rational market economics think that over time, stock pickers cannot beat the market. They may be lucky, they may occasionally be smart, but over time they will succumb to factors far more powerful—market momentum, market direction, and the statistical term called regression-toward-the-mean, which shows mathematically that given sufficient time, in nearly every category of life, the best of the best end up average. As a result, doom and gloom lay in every stock picker's future, whether it is Jay Gatsby or Warren Buffett. For these skeptical and overly rational economists and investors, the only way to bet on stocks is by betting on the market as a whole.

(For the record, I do not buy this theory. However, it would be irresponsible of me not to recount it to you.)

BUYING THE MARKET AS A WHOLE

Largely as a result of this mode of thinking, investment companies have created vehicles that behave like the market as a whole, or like a very large segment of the market. Mutual fund companies offer index funds, which are funds composed of the entire Standard & Poor's 500 group of stocks, the Dow Jones Industrial Average group of thirty stocks, the Russell 1000, and various other "baskets" and combinations, like "Spiders," which are baskets that are traded on the American Stock Exchange not as mutual funds but as individual stocks. In an up market, investors can do very well buying funds and products like these.

Index funds, in theory and practice, are less risky than individual stocks. Their risk is smaller because their performance is an *average* of the ups and downs of all the stocks in their index group. True, an index, because it is an average, will not perform as well as the best stocks, but it will not perform as poorly as the worst stocks, either, and for the same reason. Risks are spread, but by doing so, rewards are also spread since not every stock in the Dow or S&P 500 moves in the same direction at the same time. Still, the index funds had more than a couple of years in the '90s when they returned to their investors profits in excess of 20 percent.

But if you deconstruct it, these indexes performed very well during the '90s because the market as a whole performed well. That is a tautology. When the ball at Times Square dropped and we all moved collectively into the new millennium, the upward trend of the markets sputtered like a biplane running out of fuel. As a consequence, index funds performed just like the market as a whole.

The problem with strategies—all investment strategies, that is, and not just buy-the-market index strategies—is not creating them, it is deciding when to alter them. Because most strategies are based on a single investment idea coupled with a rigid plan for execution, they are difficult if not impossible to shift. And when you do change them, they lose their integrity.

A fund manager, for example, put in charge of an index fund could easily look at the thirty stocks in the Dow or the five hundred stocks in the S&P 500, and see which are performing well and which are slipping. An intelligent manager would sell the poor performers and keep the highfliers. They would do this because of their responsibility to their investors. Who cares if for a time a Dow Jones Industrial Average fund contained twenty-six stocks, instead of the usual thirty? Or a Standard & Poor's index fund contained 398 stocks instead of all 500?

But alas, the manager of an index fund cannot change the index. Each fund is governed by a set of bylaws—

whether an index or some other type of fund—that lists the types of products in which it can and cannot invest. Boards of advisors and/or directors make certain that each manager is living up to that fund's investment approach. As a result, shifts in strategy usually take a little time, and some funds, like index funds, do not have very much freedom to change what they do at all.

At its worst, managing a fund like an index is a little like sitting in the captain's seat in a plane set on autopilot as you watch the mountain shifting into your path. At its best, the manager's job resembles that of the Maytag repairman—everything on course and working well.

For those reasons, index funds perform like the market indexes. If the market slips, so do they and managers cannot jettison a stock or two that is languishing. Besides, what if the poor performers that this manager sold suddenly turned around and became highfliers? What if the manager then had to buy them back and at an inflated price? The manager would be forever playing catch-up, and much of the upside that goes with buying a market index would be lost.

While an index might mitigate the risk of picking this or that individual stock, it is still subject to what investors call market risk. In other words, although you might forgo rich rewards for greater safety by applying a buy-the-market index strategy, you are in no way immune to risks. Instead, by protecting yourself on one level, you open yourself to risks on another. Risk goes with investment. It is its handmaiden, its alter ego, its ugly step-sibling. Risk cannot ever be avoided completely. The only tried and true ways to deal with risk are to spread it over a number of products that typically react differently to economic and market conditions (stocks *and* bonds, for example) and create balanced portfolios based on those products. But even so, risk can never be vanquished completely.

THINKING LONG-TERM

Over the long haul, stocks have been one of the safest and best-performing investments. But that is a little like saying that over the long haul the weather has been really grand.

The problem with assessing any long-term activity and deciding whether it is good or bad has to do with when you begin and when you end your assessment. Since the end of World War II, the markets may have been on a longstanding upward roll, but that trend has been beset by periodic (and unpredictable!) setbacks along the way. Those bumps in the ever-upward road are really not a problem if you adopt a strategy of buy and hold and have the discipline to abide by it.

If you or a relative adopted a buy-and-hold strategy and invested in a healthy cross section of stocks or even a well-managed mutual fund at the end of World War II, each dollar invested would be worth many thousands of dollars today. Stock market analysts point out that no other category of investment—bonds, real estate, gold, silver, or stamps—has performed quite as well.

But the critical word here is *category.* Individual items—a square block of Beverly Hills real estate, a painting by Andy Warhol or Vincent van Gogh—have performed exceptionally well and have more than beat the market. But when you think of these items as members of categories, the odds favor stocks. The choice for investors then is whether to invest in individual items, trusting their own research, intelligence, savvy, and luck, or in categories, trusting someone else—a professional—to manage that investment? (I know, an investor can always do both!)

But even winning categories have losing streaks. What if you bought a stock in 1972 on the eve of one of the worst bear markets ever? Rather than watching your money multiply, you would have watched your investment disappear for a couple of years before it returned to its original investment value. If you were a patient investor with a long-term horizon, no problem. And if you bought the NASDAQ in February 2000? When would you become whole? Timing is important even if you're in it for the long haul.

There are many famous investors who are proponents of long-term investing. In the end, they say, patience wins out. Even if you bought the market in 1972, or 2000, they argue, the upward trend in the nation's growth, in the growth of the markets and in the growth of the money supply in general, would make your investment pay off. And they have the statistics to prove it.

While that may be fine for Warren Buffett, chairman of Berkshire Hathaway, perhaps one of the best long-term investors ever, what if you needed to remove your money from the market in 1973 or 2001, to buy a house or pay for a child's education or take care of an emergency? Long-term investing wins when it is really made over the long haul. Even the venerable Buffett is not entirely long-term in his approach. Sometimes Berkshire Hathaway is flush with cash due to the nature of its wholly owned businesses, which are heavily focused on insurance—an industry that either gushes with cash or is paying out heavily to cover policy holders' losses.

When it is sitting on cash, the money does not go

immediately into long-term investments. Research is required along with due diligence and an assessment of timing. When he has cash, Buffett parks it in vehicles that are appropriate for the short term. Lately, that has included silver, zero coupon bonds (they pay no interest but sell at a steep discount and can be traded before the face value is repaid by the issuer), as well as other instruments including high-risk insurance products.

But while Buffett does not eschew short-term investing when it is required due to circumstances, the core of his minority stock investments are long-term plays—American Express, Coca-Cola, Freddie Mac, Gillette, Walt Disney, Washington Post, and Wells Fargo. Other investments—the ones in which he buys all or nearly all of a company—are also long-term. When he does sell a stock, such as his holdings in U.S. Airways, he does it with an apology to shareholders for straying into areas about which his knowledge was insufficient to make money. Buffett proves that with the right strategy, tremendous discipline, a great team, and more than a little luck, you can make money no matter what the market is doing by buying individual stocks. (When embarking upon such a strategy it also helps to have an IQ like Buffett's, which is as high as his returns.)

THINKING SHORT-TERM

The other side of the coin from long-term investing is, of course, short-term investing. The philosophy here is to move into and out of the market so quickly that you can "time" your investments, thereby maximizing your gain. The short-term philosophy is exactly the opposite philosophy from the long-term investor. No surprise here. While the risks are higher because timing is everything, the rewards should also be larger because you are not locked in to a rigid formula of holding on to a stock until the end of time. If the Dow slips, you can sell whatever of it you own and cut your losses or grab your profits. If a stock like eBay or Amazon or Cisco takes off, you can catch it on the rise, whatever its category. While long-term investing is strategic, short-term investing is opportunistic and tactical. Indexes are not part of the short-term investor's mix.

The shortest of the short-term investors are the "day traders." Many day traders believe they should close out (sell) each of their positions by the end of each trading day. If they buy GE in the morning, they should have sold it by the time they call it a day. In and out of the market is what these investors believe.

Day traders come armed (literally, in at least one case) with computers linked directly to the markets via subsidiary accounts from companies with brokerage licenses. By linking directly to the market, rather than using a conventional broker to buy and sell stocks electronically, day traders can buy and sell on their own just like brokers and not have to wait while their brokers aggregate their orders with others in order to make large bids or to sell holdings in large blocks.

Day trading—at least in theory—should pay off big time. It should do so because each stock is watched like a hawk by the day trader, who sits at a computer screen and is in constant e-mail and phone contact with other traders as well. Proponents of day trading say that since a day trader watches every minute movement of a stock and can act instantly, he or she can sell when the stock begins to decline and buy it back when it turns around. That way day traders can make money if a stock moves only a penny or so—after paying trading commissions. Theoretically, a day trader can buy and sell the same stock many times in a day, profiting handsomely.

The only problem with this approach is that it requires a trader's undivided attention to succeed (as well as lots of Alka-Seltzer). And what if the trader is watching four or five stocks? Or thirty stocks? How can she track them all and make the right decision at the right time and do so on her own?

One way to manage a daily traded portfolio is with software that tracks the market's activity—or a single stock's activity—on a minute-by-minute basis. There are commercially available software packages that do this.

But even so, if your profits depend upon making a decision a second, what happens when you go to the bathroom? Or your contact lens pops out?

There are many wealthy investors, but it is difficult to find any day traders in that category.

PROFITING ON BAD NEWS

Another way to beat the market is to think short-term and leverage one position against another, via a strategy known as hedging. George Soros is to the hedge fund world what Warren Buffett is to the world of long-term investing.

Soros, operating through his Quantum Fund, has bet against such investment items as the British pound, the Malaysian ringgit, the Swedish kroner, and lots of other items. Looking at an overbought market in high-technology stocks, he bet (and lost) because he felt the market had reached its peak. He was right, but placed his bet too early.

The beauty of hedge fund investing is that it leverages one product against another. Investing the way hedge fund investors do generally requires using lots of leverage, meaning debt. If you believe shares of a stock are about to fall, you can go to your broker and ask him to execute a "short" sale for you. To do that, your broker finds someone with shares who will "lend" them to you for a small fee. (The lender is usually a brokerage firm.) They lend them to you with the understanding that they will buy them back at their current price at some point in the future.

If the agreement is for 1000 shares and the stock falls $10 a share, you go into the market as it falls, buy shares, and simultaneously sell them back to the lender at the price agreed upon in your contract. For your effort you make $10,000, less commission and the cost of the contract. If you leveraged your bet by borrowing heavily to finance your purchase, that $10,000 profit could be almost pure profit. Not a bad way to make money if a company falls out of favor.

Or, consider that if you purchased 100 shares of stock at $50 a share for $5000, and the per-share price dropped to $40, you would lose $1000. If, however, you sold the stock short at $50 and repurchased it at $40, you would have made $10 a share for a profit of $1000, less transaction fees.

The only problem with short selling is that if the stock rises, you are in trouble. You would have problems because even if the stock rose, you would still have to pay back your allotment of shares to the "lender." If the stock rose quickly, that could spell disaster. For example, if a stock rose by $10 a share above the contract price and your contract was for 1000 shares, you would have to buy 1000 shares at the going rate and give them to your broker, who would act on behalf of the lender. Your foray into hedging your downside risk would have cost you $10,000 plus commissions and the fee for the contract. If you borrowed to buy the stocks, your losses would be even more.

While hedging using short-selling techniques sounds difficult and cumbersome, it is actually quite easy to do and many billions of dollars' worth of stocks are "shorted" each day. Some people have made enormous profits hedging. In the 1980s, Feshbach Brothers, a California investment fund, made millions in profits by betting against the market. They profited tremendously when stocks collapsed on October 19, 1987, and their fund was holding dozens of short positions. The same techniques can be used for foreign stocks and even currencies. George Soros has used this technique to make billions of dollars over the years in the world's currency markets.

WHAT'S BETTER, AN UP OR A DOWN MARKET?

In 1997, Warren Buffett made quite a stir in his annual report to shareholders of Berkshire Hathaway by asking them whether they preferred a rising or a falling stock market. Most people's gut reaction is that they want a rising market. They like to see the price of their stocks go up as they check out the cumulative value of their portfolios.

According to Buffett, that is the *wrong* answer.

In his view, if you are a long-term investor buying good companies that distribute a substantial share of their profits to their shareholders via dividend payments, then what you want is a declining market.

The reason for this bit of contrary advice from the world's savviest investor is that if you are truly long-term, your aim is to always be in the market. As a result, you really never want to sell your holdings.

As a long-term investor, if you allocate a certain amount of money to invest in stocks each month, for example, and you target a few great companies for those investment dollars, then as the market falls the money you allocate to purchase stock will buy more shares. If those stocks return a more-or-less constant dividend to their shareholders, then the real return on your investment actually goes up as the price of the shares goes down.

Consider how simply and elegantly this works.

If you pay $10 for a share of stock and it returns a dividend of $1 per share per year, you are making 10 percent on your money by holding those shares. If the stock goes down to $8 a share and you buy more shares, the $1 dividend means your return has risen to 12.5 percent. In a falling market, as you average the cost of your old $10 shares with your new $8 shares, the average cost of shares comes down while the dividend remains constant. If you put these two trends together—and if you continue buying shares in the declining market (and you are buying those shares in great companies)—your overall returns will continue to increase.

True, if the price of the shares you bought for $10 went up to $12, the return on your initial investment in the stock would have increased by 20 percent. However, since you are keeping those shares rather than selling them, those "unrealized gains" do you very little good. In addition, the $1 dividend per share means that your return on the stock has fallen from 10 percent to 8.33 percent. And, if you buy more shares, the same money will buy you 20 percent fewer shares.

According to Buffett, the only time you ever really want the market to rise is when you decide to cash out.

Although there are a myriad of ways to approach the market, one thing is certain. The shorter your investment time frame, the more attention the market will demand of you. Buying for the long haul means that the market's overall trend is in your favor. It also means that the demands on your psyche are far fewer than if you were a short-term investor.

True, many short-term investors have done remarkably well. The truth is, however, that those who have done the best do it for a living. They sit in front of the screen all day and have their pagers and cell phones on all night. They are backed up by research departments and analysts. They have software that is developed especially for them. When the market moves—here or anywhere—they are on alert. Because they must always be alert to market shifts, they are about as much fun to be with as an obstetrician who is always on call. And yes, the ones who make money through short-term investments are probably also geniuses.

CHAPTER SIX

The Difference Between Price and Value

While it is tempting to focus exclusively on the emotional aspects of the market—which I have been doing painstakingly and with sufficient repetition so as to convince you of even my weakest and least tenable points—I would be remiss were I not to at least note that the markets also have a rational side. If I am right in my contention that markets move on sentiment, individual stocks do not necessarily follow suit. Some stocks and even bonds are priced with a high regard for their underlying value while others are priced emotionally. To put it another way, some prices are set because of well-supported hunches about the future while others are set because of great sales pitches and some wild dreams. Telling which from which is an art.

The market is a phenomenon of aggregation. As such, like baseball, it is not so much about individual plays as it is about the statistics of a season or a career. A world's hopes and fears collide each day the moment the market opens. When there is agreement about the future—more hope than dread, more dread than hope—the market moves in the direction of whichever predominates. Sideways markets—with short periods of ups followed by short periods of downs—indicate that people do not really see eye-to-eye about tomorrow.

Even when the investing "masses" are in agreement, they can be rational or irrational. Let's look at two of my favorite examples.

In October 1929 when the market plunged, the world economy, just like the Wile E. Coyote cartoon character, strayed too far over the edge of the cliff. After pausing in mid-air, the economy collapsed along with the market.

The reasons for the plunge were entirely rational. *It should have plunged!* In fact, if investors had been paying attention to what they were doing, rather than following the herd, they could have prevented most of their own losses. The signals were everywhere.

The reason for the plunge was that after World War I, Germany, which lost the war, was forced by the victors to pay massive reparations for the havoc it had caused. The conditions of those payments were onerous—they amounted to a tax by the victors on a great many commercial activities conducted within Germany—and some savvy observers said as much. John Maynard Keynes, still a young man and not yet the towering figure in economics that he would become, wrote that the agreement covering reparations might spell disaster for the world.

By putting such difficult and ultimately untenable conditions on Germany, the world's dominant powers created a situation in which economic weakness and instability would be located in the very heart of Europe. Germany's massive reparation payments meant that it had no money to invest in its future and very little to distribute to its companies and people. While Europe rebuilt and grew in the aftermath of World War I, Germany became mired in unemployment and poverty.

At the same time, the United States, Britain, and France, the recipients of Germany's war-time payments, grew dependent on that money. As a result, when Germany defaulted on its payments, it threw the rest of Europe into an economic tailspin and damaged the United States as well.

While this was occurring on a global basis, investors in the United States were borrowing heavily to underwrite their stock market bets. By borrowing from banks either directly or indirectly to buy stocks, unwise investors were using the nation's savings to keep the stock market rising.

When stocks fell, it not only wiped out a huge share of the nation's investment capital, it also wiped out the nation's savings.

Why do I recount these events? I do so because all of them were reported in the newspapers, magazines, radio programs, and newsreels of the day. Had investors looked at the world beyond the markets they would have been able to see that world unravel. As a result, staying in the market was irrational, even though it was rising handsomely during the 1920s; pulling out money would have been rational, which everyone did on the same October day in 1929.

By contrast, the next biggest stock market collapse, which occurred in October 1987, was an example of the world undergoing an irrational case of the jitters. The pessimists swayed the optimists, but not for very long. People were worried, but the underlying economic conditions of the world were terrifically strong. Aside from a short recession in 1991, the world experienced almost a decade-long period of growth, measured along any economic axis—from economic expansion, to job creation, to productivity gains, to increased levels of home ownership, to increasing levels of household wealth, to wage growth, and so on. The 1987 crash was the portent of nothing really very bad. There was no depression that followed it and few people lost their jobs. If you took your money out of the market, you lost big-time. If you left it in, over time, the worth of your investments would have multiplied. Unlike the 1929 debacle, the 1987 collapse meant that people suddenly and violently agreed in an irrational way.

AGGREGATING DIVERSE PRODUCTS

Because markets are large aggregations of behavior, they affect a large number of individual financial instruments. But the behaviors that markets aggregate are actually rather simple—the decision to buy or sell. These binary decisions focus only on the sale or purchase of individual stocks, bonds, options, indexes, and so on, but by doing so determine where vast amounts of capital are deposited. The macro-movements of capital reflect sentiment, but the micro-decisions that underpin them reflect other things as well.

Because the market operates on a number of levels, there is often a disconnect between the movement of a single stock and the movement of the market in general or even the movement of a sector. The markets in this respect resemble the *wave* pattern that can ripple spontaneously through seventy thousand or more fans at a football game. You may go to a game (face painted, shirt off, belly full of

beer, wearing a funny hat) and stand up with your arms in the air trying to start the wave. Most of the time you will be greeted with yells of "Down in front!" But every once in a while, if you are lucky, other fans will stand and then quickly sit to join in the wave pattern you started.

If you study the videotape of the wave carefully, you will see that not everyone stands up, that some people stand at the wrong time, that some people remain standing, that some seats are empty. Looking at an individual fan does not give you a true picture of the whole. You need to look at the wave from a distance and without the distraction of examining how each fan behaves.

If you buy the market as a whole through indexes, spiders, or some other tool, you are doing the equivalent of betting on the wave. If you buy a mutual fund, you are doing the equivalent of buying a "section" of the seats at the stadium and hoping the fans in those seats will stand up at the right time. If you buy an individual stock, you are doing the equivalent of betting on a single football fan and hoping he or she will stand up at the right time.

FIGURING VALUE

This is not a book about what to invest in, but it is a book about how to *think* about investing. To do that, let us return to what we discussed earlier—the concept of *value*.

Markets are designed and run to determine price. Sometimes the price and value of a company are the same and can be arrived at simply by looking at the price of a stock, adding up the number of shares, and multiplying that number against the price. The product of doing that bit of elementary math gives you what is called market

cap, or market capitalization. Market capitalization is the value of all outstanding stock.

It is quite rare, however, for a company's market cap to be equal to its *value*. Market cap is a snapshot in time— *today!* If you wanted to buy a company, filed the proper papers with the regulators, and attempted to buy each share of stock that is outstanding, you could obtain the company for its market cap. Generally, though, when a company is in play and investors know someone wants to buy their shares, they hold back and wait for a higher price. That price may be determined by the market, or the acquirer may meet with the management and the board of directors of the "target" company and negotiate a price. When that happens, shareholders must vote on the offer.

Sometimes, during weeks of haggling between the acquirer and the board and management of the target company, share prices fluctuate. Outside investors, wanting to cash in on the well-publicized deal, rush in and buy the stock, and by doing so bid up its price. Then, when the deal takes longer than expected, these impatient investors sell their shares and the overall value of the stock falls.

Value is not an absolute, like the speed of light, the temperature at which water boils, or Superman's supremacy over the evil menace Lex Luthor. Instead, value is relative and it is different things to different people. The underlying element that determines value is the degree to which the thing valued is also *needed*.

Because value is different from price, the savviest investors are the ones who can calculate the value of a company, its stocks and bonds and the derivatives of those instruments, and relate that to the price at which these items trade. From that it makes sense to conclude that when price is higher than value, sell, and when value is

less than price, buy. Keep in mind that if those times when price and value diverged were easy to discover, every investor would be rich.

THREE TYPES OF VALUE

There are several types of value. In addition to market value, or market cap, companies have what is called strategic value. This is the value one company sets on another for purely business purposes. For example, a company that makes components for the computer industry might value its rival manufacturer higher than the price of its stock. It would do this because an analysis of the two businesses might reveal that there would be significant cost savings if the two companies combined. It would get those savings by combining the marketing and sales forces of the two companies and by combining the manufacturing operations. If by doing that the company realized higher combined revenues at combined lesser costs, then there might be significant strategic value in excess of the price of the stock.

Strategic opportunities are not necessarily open to individual investors unless they buy an interest in companies such as I just mentioned. Cashing in on strategic value is not even necessarily open to funds.

Once, in another life, when I was a partner of Michael Milken's, one of the most gifted, maligned, misunderstood, and brilliant financiers of the twentieth century, we attempted to purchase a major publishing company. Combined with our own firm's resources, we were able to raise funds to allow us to bid $4.2 billion for the enterprise we were seeking. Our aim was to transform the publishing company into a powerhouse for the on-line distribution of content. But we had no other publishing assets at the time and therefore could not combine the operations of the company we were seeking with those of any other publishing firm. As a result, we had only the most minimal opportunity to cut costs, while an existing publisher would have been able to determine how savings might occur from combining things like computer systems, distribution systems, sales forces, marketing programs, and even printing. True, savings occur when people are let go. But even more savings can occur because of new efficiencies coming from the combined companies' larger scale. (I should point out that these efficiencies are not always easy to achieve, that many companies do not get them, and that the ones that do often do not achieve them until they invest even *more* money in the combined companies.)

Anyway, as soon as we put in our $4.2-billion final bid, a European publishing company entered in a bid for $4.6 billion *plus*.

Mike, a math genius who could do intricate math puzzles, problems, and tricks in his head (many of which amazed me, many of which annoyed me), did all the sums. Even with his formidable financial mind, his business sense, and his daring approach, we were unable to do an analysis that made a higher bid work for us. The problem we had in acquiring that company was that we were up against an investor for whom it made sense to pay a premium to acquire the company based on its strategic value.

Another type of value is *book* value. This is an easily arrived at number that requires only a little math to do. You look at a company's balance sheet, add up its assets, and subtract from that all of its liabilities, including its liabili-

ties of outstanding preferred stock—which is considered
for this exercise to be a type of loan. You then divide that
number by the total number of shares outstanding. By
doing so, you arrive at the company's book value per share.
At first glance, book value looks like the key to understanding the disparity between price and value. A share of
GE might trade in the $55 range, while its book value is
listed in the $13 range. Now we are getting somewhere!

Oh no we're not. Book value is actually a somewhat
misleading number from an investment point of view. The
reason why it misleads is that companies carry on their
books the value of their assets at the time they were
acquired. As a result, the value of a factory (or a piece of
real estate or equipment) that cost $10 million to build in
1985 and $6 million to update in 1996 might actually be
worth far more than the $16 million that is reflected on
the balance sheet. As a result, book value is not very useful for investors when attempting to discern the difference
between a company's stock price and its real value.

Now let us come back to a concept of value that we
touched on in a previous chapter and that bears further
development. This is the notion of value as measured by
the ability of a company to create a return on shareholder
equity.

In its simplest form, this type of value is simply earning per share as a percentage of the price of a share. From
this point of view, if a share costs $10 and its dividend to
shareholders is $1, its return on shareholder equity is 10
percent.

Some companies use return on shareholder equity as
a measuring rod. At Progressive Insurance, an innovative
insurer in Cleveland, return on shareholder equity is used
as an investment tool. According to Progressive's annual

report, "Our goal is to achieve an after-tax return on shareholders' equity over a five-year period that is at least 15 percentage points greater than the rate of inflation (measured by the consumer price index, which was 3.4% in 2000, and averaged 2.5% over the past five years and 2.7% over the past ten years). If we believe we can earn such a profit, we will invest in business operations. If we do not believe we can earn such a profit, we will return underleveraged capital to our investors." For the managers at Progressive, using that measure ensures that they treat the shareholder as the owner by deciding upon acquisitions based upon how much those investments will return to the shareholder's wallet. Ten percent is nothing to sneeze at, as the saying goes, especially in the Greenspan era when banks routinely pay interest of less than 5 percent and Treasury notes pay less than 6 percent.

But to find out whether an investment is good and the value is right, we need to take a moment to discuss discounted cash flow analysis, or DCF, in a deeper fashion than we previously did. DCF is the backbone of the way in which Warren Buffett invests; it is the way MBAs value companies to buy. And, while it sounds complicated, it is actually not too difficult a concept to use.

The question DCF is designed to answer is, What's a guy or gal really supposed to pay for a stock? Or, How much is that share *really* worth versus how high it is priced? The way DCF answers that question is to see how much cash a stock will produce over time and discount that flow back to the future. If you are able to *reduce* the amount of cash thrown off today by a number that is relevant over the long haul, then you can arrive at a price for the stock that makes at least a modicum of sense.

To do a DCF, you need to know what's called the stock's expected rate of return, the time over which you will own the stock, and the final value of the investment. Let's look at each element individually.

The final value of a stock is easy to determine. The easiest way to do so is to look up a stock's P/E value. What is P/E value? It is the ratio of price to earnings per share. A stock that sells for $10 with a P/E ratio of 10 has earnings of $1 per share. Traditionally, the stock market has an overall P/E ratio of around 18–22. (Yes, there really are computer-assisted nerds who add that up and do the math for the thousands of stocks traded to find the entire market's price-to-earnings ratio!) Anyway, there are several ways to figure out final value; using P/E ratios is only one.

The easiest way to get the final value is to assume that a company will earn $1 a share and that earnings due to the growth of the economy, increased efficiencies, new technology, and new managerial approaches will grow nicely for five years. Let's also assume the company will have a P/E ratio of 10, to be on the conservative side, in five years when you want to sell the stock. The simplest formula for figuring out the final share price will be to assume the P/E ratio will remain at 10 and that earnings will grow to $2 a share. If we figure a P/E of 10, we are guessing that the final share price will be $20.

If we want an 8-percent return on our investment in order to beat the safest of all investments, the Treasury note with its 5.5-percent return, and do so with enough added upside profit to offset the risk of investing in the market instead of government bonds, then we take our expected final price of the stock and discount it back to its present value. The formula for doing this is $20, less

8 percent per year for five years. A stock that costs $20 a share in five years should cost about $13.50 today, if we are to make 8 percent a year on our money.

The point of this exercise is that it shows how long-term investors think. They look at a company and try to figure out its current value by guessing (in an educated manner) about its future worth. The math they employ to do this is a little like the way people think about bonds. How much do you have to pay for a bond that will be worth $20 in five years and will pay you interest of about 15 percent a year? The answer: about $13.50. By thinking of stocks in the same way, and by upping their hoped-for returns to compensate for risk, they can calculate what they think is a reasonable price to pay for a stock based upon its value, not its gyrating price. Using DCF is not a sure thing. It assumes a lot. First, it assumes you know the final value of a stock. (We're back to guessing games regarding sentiment and the ups and downs of the overall market and the sectors that make it up.)

Stock market analysts figure out risk with a term they call beta. The way they measure risk is in no way absolute, but relative. What beta does is look at how a stock moves against the market. If the market rises by 10 percent, a stock with a beta of 2 is likely to rise by 20. Those are great gains. However, the flip side of that number is that if the market falls by 10 percent, a stock with a beta of 2 is likely to fall by 20 percent. Beta is a measure of how risky a stock is relative to the market as a whole.

In addition to risk, to figure out a final value, you need to understand how much a company's earnings will grow over time. This excludes start-ups and even young companies because they have no histories of earnings growth. As a result, calculating the final price is usually something that investors can do with reliability only when they study old-line companies. For that reason, Warren Buffett, a proponent of DCF, does not invest in new companies or in start-ups. There is simply no way to really forecast their future earnings. As a result, he is "relegated" to investing in old-line firms with predictable returns. (Let's not weep for Warren, however, just because he has to forgo investing in leading-edge companies. His returns speak for themselves.)

PRICE AND VALUE

No method of calculating value works forever. Even Buffett has picked some losers over the years and no one can pick winners forever. However, the mind-set investors should adopt—and this is a book about mind-set—is to have an investing philosophy that balances the rational with the irrational ways in which the market works.

The experts say that the easiest way to lay off risk is to buy a stock index. The next best way is to buy a basket of stocks for the long term and hold them. After that, the next best way to invest is to diversify among stocks, bonds, and other products.

Over time, stocks are the best *category* of investment, but not every time. Over time, government and blue-chip corporate bonds are the safest, but not the best, investments. Balancing the two together provides the best mix of safety and yield.

And, overall, the best method for selecting stocks is to use DCF.

There are several ways to calculate DCF. There are CD-ROMs, on-line courses, and books about the best way to do the calculations. If you are patient and careful, DCF could be the way to go. But if you are lazy—like almost everyone who invests—you may set a goal of using DCF as a tool to make your bets, but never employ it. For that reason, there are DCF resources you can purchase or get for free. For starters, have a look at such on-line newsletters as *Investopedia,* investment sites like Motley Fool, programs like RealDCF (software for the real estate industry), and Investit (an on-line calculator for most industries). You can also get programs for your PC or Mac from CostBenefit.com, an on-line service. But if you really want to use this nifty investment tool, Hewlett-Packard sells calculators like the HP10b, which is programmed to do different types of DCF calculations.

It is worth checking them out.

CHAPTER SEVEN

Respecting the Markets

As you can see from the previous discussion, I am partial to the discounted cash flow method of determining the difference—and therefore the opportunity—that results from the gap between price and value. But don't let your eyes gloss over as you go through the DCF section. It is not difficult to employ and in fact is a very useful tool for determining the right price for nearly anything that is expected to appreciate in value in the future. It takes only a good calculator to perform some DCF magic, and some even come programmed with formulas that do the work for you.

The DCF method can be used not only for buying stocks, but also for purchasing houses, land, and other items that have the potential to grow in value. (Forget about using DCF to justify to your partner, mate, mom, or self the purchase of a new Porsche, Ferrari, or Lamborghini. Forget about it for justifying the purchase of that Chanel suit or Brioni jacket.) Investments (so called) in assets that depreciate over time or that waste away, evaporate, or are consumed are best made with the heart, the palette, or your aesthetic sense. Life is as much about having fun as it is about saving or making money. Rarely are we lucky enough to find an investment that is also an *experience* we can enjoy. (Perhaps owning a share in a winning racehorse like Seabiscuit or a painting by van Gogh or an apartment on Park Avenue qualifies.) But for the most part, investments exist outside of the realm of enjoyment or even outside of the realm of experience. Case in point: Warren Buffett, who has employed the DCF method to make investment decisions, has his largest holdings concentrated in the insurance industry.

There are a number of other elements to think about in regard to value and price that should be considered when it comes to making decisions about investments.

This is a book about how to think about markets. It is structured that way because it is my contention that if you have a clear understanding of how the markets work, the decisions that you make based upon that understanding will be rewarded. I am not saying that every decision an informed person makes will be right. But knowledge and information are what tip the balance in the investor's favor. When Arthur Levitt was head of the Securities and Exchange Commission during the Clinton administrations, he said that his job was to protect the informed investor, the one who works hard to make the right decision at the right time based upon the right information. And while Mr. Levitt's job was to protect all investors from abuse, he had very little patience for investors who did not do their homework. Intuition, which can be a powerful force in your life, is not sufficient to determine where to put your IRA. Rather, you need to use your head. If you are not prepared to do the work, you must be prepared to suffer the pain.

The economy—*the markets*—are very big and very complex and they are utterly and completely without the capacity to forgive. If you make a major mistake, you risk losing a major amount of your money. Once your money is gone it is, well, *gone.* That's it! When it comes to punishing bad decisions, the markets are the most democratic of all institutions. They do not care about gender, race, religion, or sexual orientation, whether you are an atheist or a true believer, or whether you've been naughty or nice.

I have no idea whether the markets respond to prayer, but I know they do not respond to worry. I also know that they do not in any way respect whether or not you are a deserving individual. The markets respect neither widows nor orphans when it comes to separating them from their metaphorical shirts, blouses, and skirts. And markets do not respect intention, nor do they respect the goodness, depth, or wisdom of your heart. Poets and pedants are both fair game.

The only thing the markets respect is a decision to buy or sell. From my own experience and from the experience of people I respect, I can say that the best decisions are made when the mind is filled with the kind of information that comes from working out an investment strategy that is highly disciplined but not so rigid that it is set in concrete. The best of these decisions is made when an investor has set clear investment goals and has identified as many obstacles as possible between him and his goals. If you won't or can't do the work, your only fallback should be to pick some highly rated mutual funds and leave it at that. But even *that* takes work.

Among the chief obstacles to making good investment decisions is apathy. Because even the best market information can be—how shall I say this?—confusing, poorly written, esoteric, and just plain boring; it can put you to sleep. Making a date to sit down with friends or with your significant other to talk about your portfolio is one of those dates that is a top candidate to be canceled or postponed indefinitely. Almost anything in life has a higher priority.

To counter apathy, I suggest you do two things. First, you can keep a running chart of the value of your investments on a weekly basis. I don't mean looking at your portfolio on-line each day and either celebrating your wins or wringing your hands. I mean charting your progress using a meaningful time frame—weekly, for example. Keep the chart up to date, use graph paper or do it on your computer screen, but show the value of your investments as a line that goes up or down. The act of updating your chart will keep you focused and will keep you from falling asleep at the switch. It will also ease you out of a false sense of security and visibly warn you of problems.

The other method for combating apathy is to spend some time each week studying the markets. I am not talking about reading the newspaper or watching CNN. I am talking about reading books and articles and while doing so making certain that you understand each term that is used. The financial world is always inventing new words and concepts. You practically need to read about the finances with a copy of *The Portable MBA* or some other reference book on your lap. Knowledge and a good scorecard are handy tools for combating financial apathy.

END OF THE BUSINESS CYCLE. YEAH, SURE!

No investment should ever be made without a thorough consideration of the economic context surrounding it. I know this may sound like a pretty abstract statement, but I do not mean it to be so. Investments that work in lean times are not necessarily the same as those that work in times of plenty.

In the 1990s, a number of economists stated quite publicly that the business cycle had in effect been repealed. They said that new technologies would ensure that productivity would be on the rise . . . *forever.* With every worker producing more each hour, thanks to new technologies, salaries *and* profits could go up at the same time. As a result the nation's standard of living would also rise. And, sure enough, after stagnating for twenty years, personal income, adjusted for inflation, began to rise.

At the same time, globalization meant that workers from around the world would be producing more of the goods we consumed with two beneficial effects. First, low-wage textile and other workers in places like Sri Lanka, Haiti, or Belize would see their incomes grow and would eventually become consumers of the products and services we produced. The sons and daughters of Sri Lankan textile workers would soon be buying laptop computers made with Intel chips and running software from Microsoft. These same workers would be talking on cell phones made by Motorola or on cell phones using chips made by other companies in the United States.

In the long run, richer foreign workers would buy more American goods of all kinds, which would help our economy. In the short run, foreign workers would exert a powerful downward pressure on prices by working for far less money than their American counterparts. With cheaper labor, foreign factories could produce goods for less than in the United States. DaimlerChrysler, Ford, GM, IBM, Dell, Boeing, and nearly every other American company uses components made globally. Wal-Mart, Kmart, The Gap, and every other retailer sell goods made internationally. In fact, most of world trade is no longer in finished goods, like computers, but in the components that make those finished goods. In addition, the overwhelming majority of trade is no longer between different companies but between different divisions of multinational companies.

Because American companies must compete with foreign companies using higher-priced American workers, the economists argue, they have been forced to automate their processes and invest heavily in new processes and in computers. Investments like that have paid off handsomely and are generally believed to have been the reason that productivity increased in the 1990s. If American workers produce 10 percent more per hour each year for the same cost, they can compete with workers who are earning less money than they do but are operating far less efficiently.

For those reasons a number of influential economists have bet their reputations on the New Economy and have stated that the prices of goods will remain flat while productivity, wages, and profits will soar. With those factors in effect, they have said there is no way but up.

And yet, as the events of the early 2000s have shown, the business cycle has not been repealed, chaos can reign, unforeseen circumstances can play their hand in history, wars can ignite, tempers can flare, and for every up there is, eventually, a down.

The reason that I point this out is to suggest that while the economy is a gigantic, complex system, with the markets acting as electronic distribution points for the world's aggregate buying power, it is not a robot. The markets are human creations and are therefore subject to human frailties. As long as people are on board this planet, they will need to allocate goods and services as well as risk. As long as people live here, the markets will reflect their points of view. Let me state it one more time: For every up, there will be a down, as surely as the day follows the night.

This does not mean that every time of prosperity will of necessity be followed by a time of depression. As an optimist, I believe that prosperity is on the rise globally and that it will continue to be so as long as people are free to pursue their own interests and are allowed to be productive. The winds of economic growth have been blowing for a very long time.

And yet, while the human spirit is indefatigable, tyrants abound and the freedom to pursue creativity in the material realm is not a given; it must be continually won. Yet, in most of the world, the bias is toward the creative and the dynamic and toward economic growth. If people are allowed to be free, they would be far more focused on the future than on the present or the past. If people are allowed to pursue their dreams, the bias is toward expansion.

Since the end of World War II, more than two billion people around the world have been lifted out of abject poverty and into the ranks of the middle class. This has been the case on every continent where the markets have been allowed to work in an environment free from war. People of all backgrounds and all cultures have prospered.

Where there has been a significant investment in human capital, through education and training, and in social capital, through the creation of well-designed institutions, the market has worked its magic in amazing ways. Where countries have faltered it has been because they have failed to invest in human capital and in strong, market-oriented institutions. Since the unit of action in a markets economy is the individual—*all decisions are arrived at through choice and negotiation*—they are the heartiest and most robust of economies. Since everyone has a stake, everyone shares in the risk and everyone has a stab at gaining the rewards.

But while the direction is up, no trend proceeds without at least momentary interruptions. Periods of growth are followed by periods of fatigue. Stocks rise higher, then plunge, then rise higher again. A sailboat, to venture upwind, must tack to the starboard, then to the port, again and again, if it is to reach its destination.

In the long term, as John Maynard Keynes said with all the doom, gloom, and gravitas of a great economist, we are all dead. But in truth, the long term is a lot shorter than it used to be and we all live a lot longer than in Keynes' day.

What I mean by that is that while it took nearly a century to build the railroads and to lace the nation together with wires carrying electricity, telegraph, and telephone, it has taken a far shorter period to knit the nation together even more tightly with radio, TV, cable, cellular phones, computers, and the Internet. This is true because one infrastructure builds upon another. With the railroads in place, massive electric generators could be moved anywhere they were needed. With electricity coursing through the nation's grid, radios, TVs, and computers could be powered up. With computers and telephones in place, the Internet could be built. With telephone switching stations in place, cell phone towers could be made practical. As a consequence, the long term is shorter than it used to be and people, in a single lifetime, can live through several different eras. Like the layered ruins of an archaeological dig, each new technology is built upon the previous ones. New technologies built upon today's formidable infrastructure will become tomorrow's engines of growth.

So the long term is shorter. But even more important, when I say economic context, I mean the overall level of prices and their rate of increase over time. We have already seen how globalization keeps companies from raising prices. But if prices were absolutely stable, which means a zero rate of inflation, then money left in a bank account at 3.2 percent compounded annually—and no risk—would do just fine for most of us, assuming we put away a sufficient amount of money each month. The math on compounding does astounding things and we should pay attention to it.

But in reality inflation is never zero and prices are never stable across the board. Prices rise by some measure and they do so every year. In the '90s, they rose by 3 to 4 percent a year and they did so unevenly. The price of food was pretty stable; the price of oil, gas, steel, and other commodities was flat to down; the price of big-ticket consumer goods like cars was flat; the prices of computers rose but so did their power; so the amount paid per processing unit was down.

Even so, housing rose far more than the overall 3- to 4-percent inflation rate. In fact, in some regions of the country, it increased from 10 to 30 percent or even more in a single year. Statistics are averages, which means they are a composite picture of real life. With regard to these statistics, economists have a joke: If your head is in the oven and your feet are in a freezer, on average your temperature is just fine.

The amount of money in circulation is the ocean upon which all of the economy's boats float. It is hard for the Fed to control the money supply precisely. The amount of money in circulation rises and falls depending upon how much people borrow or pay back through the banking system. It changes in relation to their purchases and sales of Treasury bonds. It also changes when the Fed buys or sells bonds in a big way or when it moves the levers it controls, such as short-term interest rates, which discourage or encourage banks, businesses, and individuals to borrow. To slow inflation by raising interest rates—or to jump-start growth by lowering interest rates—is a lot more art than science. As a result, the economy is always a little out of whack—which is one reason why it is so difficult to forecast the future.

MONEY AND PRICE

For the most part, the amount of money in circulation determines prices overall. Too much money means prices rise too quickly, too little means that prices don't rise at all, or even fall. But there are other, lesser factors that determine price, too, like demand versus supply. Some demand factors have macro-economic impact. An increase in the demand for oil (or a shortfall in supplies) drives prices up across the board for everything. Rising oil prices do this because almost every aspect of the economy uses oil at least in some way. Worker shortages also send prices higher since wage increases are often not confined to a single industry.

And yet, there are some economists who argue that oil prices rise not simply because OPEC says they should rise, but also because the folks who manage the world's central banks have printed too much money. With too much money in circulation, each dollar buys less. Since oil is priced in dollars, the buying power of the world's oil producers goes down. To rehabilitate their buying power, the world's oil producers raise the price of oil. After all, if the price of a Lincoln Navigator goes up, the people who run OPEC must either raise their prices in order to keep their garages full or pump more barrels of oil out of their wells.

The same is true for labor. Many union organizers argue that they strike not because they are greedy, but because the price of goods has risen too high too quickly. Auto workers making $39 an hour cannot afford to live the way they did if prices rise as a result of too much money in circulation. For them to buy their Lincoln Navigators means more hours of overtime every time prices rise.

Seen from this perspective, rising prices and rising wage rates are not the cause of inflation but the effect of a monetary system that is either poorly managed or out of control.

One other point. When an economy becomes over-heated, when it is growing faster than its ability to produce the goods and services people want, prices also rise. But there is an argument over this as well. For years economists thought a mature economy, like ours, could grow at only about 2.5 percent. But now they believe it can grow faster because of the growth of productivity. But even this number is looked at askance by some. After all, if an economy is growing swiftly, wouldn't manufacturers add production lines and wouldn't banks automate their services and wouldn't consulting firms hire more people? In fact, they do. Even the venerable Harley-Davidson motorcycle company added new production lines to meet the increased demand for its products in the 1990s. True, it did not move swiftly—sort of rumbled to its decision— but it added lines. What company in its right mind would turn away business? If money is stable and interest rates are stable, companies can afford to expand. In my view, thinking of a speed limit for the United States economy— with its dynamism and entrepreneurial flare—is out- moded. As long as money is stable and prices are flat, people will invest in growth.

Because money determines price, an individual's investments (or a company's investments, for that matter) have to beat the inflation rate or they are useless. With strong, clear-headed Federal Reserve chairmen like Paul Volker and Alan Greenspan, inflation has been kept low with the result being growth.

So the first economic *bogie* (what does that uncouth little word really mean?) for investing is the inflation rate. When it is high, investors have to think differently from when inflation is low. How hard was that to figure out?

The second bogie investors must consider before using DCF or any other investment tool is what some peo- ple call the risk-free rate. This is an important concept. The benchmark for risk-free investments is the thirty-year U.S. Treasury bond, which has always paid off its investors on time. Government bonds from other coun- tries can be quite risky, however, for countless reasons. In the United States and elsewhere, corporate bonds can be dubious as well, since they are tied to the fortunes of an individual company. As a result, U.S. Treasuries are the tried and true benchmark for a risk-free investment. They are the world-wide standard. The point of picking a benchmark is that whatever you buy that is riskier than Treasuries has to pay more than Treasuries to make the promise of a reward worth the risk.

If you are buying stocks, and you use DCF to analyze a company and it produces a yield of 7 percent, with a beta of 2, you have to ask yourself if the risk of owning that stock, which can fall at twice the rate of the market, makes the return worth it.

The way to answer that question logically is to look at the risk-free yield on Treasuries. If they are earning nearly the same rate or close to your investment, why bother with anything else? It just doesn't make much sense to add a heap of risk to your portfolio in exchange for a percent or two of potential reward.

This was very clear to me when I met with a friend who runs a hedge fund. He wanted me to invest in his fund. The fund, which bets on certain stocks falling, others rising, and everything in between, turned in a wonderful performance of 20 percent a year during the 1990s. But it is hugely risky and heavily leveraged.

When I met with the manager in late 2001, the fund had yielded a return of only 3 percent for the entire year. Granted, it was a difficult year, with stocks falling broadly, corporate earnings down, uncertainty over the attack on the World Trade Center, and many other factors. Before we met to talk about the fund, I checked out the paper and saw that two-year Treasuries were paying 2.97 percent! It took only a second for me to decide not to invest in my friend's offering. His performance so far was only slightly higher than that of a Treasury bond while the risk was off the charts. True, his fund might turn around before the year ends and turn in a performance in line with the previous year's result. However, with so much uncertainty and so little proven results, I bought bonds instead.

Since the long run is shorter than it used to be, I can sell my two-year bonds whenever I want and use the proceeds to do whatever I want, smart, dumb, or dumber. If my friend's fund begins to yield a return at, say, 13 percent, I may just sell those bonds and invest in the fund. At that level, the risk may be worth the potential of a far greater reward. But for now, why forgo the safety of the benchmark of risk-free investing for a promise that may never come?

That is what the markets are all about—moving around your money to achieve your strategic aims and your investment goals.

CHAPTER EIGHT

How Information Moves Markets

Imagine once more that stiff-legged Soviets troops are marching in Red Square. Their high black boots are polished, their uniforms are pressed, their dark green tanks, missiles, and half-tracks are on parade. At the viewing stands, the Soviet elite stares cold-eyed at the show beneath them, a vivid dramatization of the Evil Empire's Cold War might.

But in the factories, they are telling jokes like this one: An American manager walks into a vast Soviet truck manufacturing plant and looks around. "This is quite impressive," he says to his Soviet counterpart. "How many people work here?" The Soviet manager looks at the shop floor, then looks back at the American. "About half," the Soviet says.

At many Soviet factories, workers would show up long enough to buy cheap vodka and other black-market goods and then depart. At others, managers would show up long enough to drape a sweater or coat on their desk chairs to make it look as if they were at a meeting somewhere else in the building. Having advertised their presence, the managers would depart their worksites only to conduct business in the black market. Alcoholism and absenteeism took a huge toll on the old Soviet-era factories.

No one knew how bad it really was.

Back then, when I first met Abel Aganbegyan, chief economic advisor to reform-minded President Gorbachev, I asked him to name his most pressing concern.

"No data," the big man said simply. "We are creating a set of reforms without understanding how bad or big the problem is."

Mr. Aganbegyan, an economist trained in the intricate anti-market thinking of Karl Marx, explained that because the Soviet Union had lied about its rate of economic growth for so long, no one knew for certain how big and powerful its economy really was. As a result, none of the economic doctors knew whether to prescribe a thimbleful of medicine or do transplant surgery. Among economists, there was even more discord than usual. I recall one economist—Stanislav Shatalin—gaining support for a five-hundred-day transition to capitalism. Five hundred days! A decade later and Russia is still limping along.

Because there was so little readily available information about the economy, one early reformist leader was Yuri Andropov, a former head of the KGB, the Soviet spy agency. Among the ruling elite, it was theorized that if no one in government or industry knew for sure what was happening in the economy, perhaps the KGB did. And yet, according to Aganbegyan, not even the KGB was keeping track, even though it had thousands of clandestine operatives at home and abroad. Soviet politicians, bureaucrats, and managers had lied so often and for so long about that country's economic performance, that no one knew the truth.

"We really thought at first all we needed to do was increase the production of machine tools and that would be it," Aganbegyan said. "We really thought we were just a few steps behind the United States and the West. But what we found when we started to assemble data was that we had an economic disaster in our country. A real economic disaster."

Why bring this up now?

The market is a mechanism for setting prices and spreading risk. It is where transactions are conducted, which is how those prices are set. The market cannot work its wonders without the right kind of information. How can you transact business if you don't really understand what is going on?

The first area of information that the market requires is internal to companies and deals with their performance, which is the content aspect. But internal information is also important contextually. If you are deciding to buy a stock, you need to know how the issuing company performs. Without accurate information about the market and its conditions (Is there sufficient capital? Are stocks undervalued or overvalued given historical criteria? Are certain sectors favored? What is the overall mood of the investing public?) it is difficult to determine the difference between price and value. Without good information regarding these factors, we are no better off than the old-time Soviets.

Internally, market-economy companies need to know how they are performing across a broad spectrum of functions in addition to revenue or sales. They need to know the cost of producing the goods and services they sell, including the cost of fielding a sales force, putting together marketing programs, paying the rent, and accounting for other types of overhead.

Companies also need to understand the rate of return on the money they have invested in their business and how much money is tied up in their unsold inventories of goods. They need to keep track of how much is owed to them—over the long and short hauls—and how much they owe to others and at what rates. Companies need to understand the value of their assets (everything from their real estate to their brand) and whether those assets are appreciating or depreciating. They need to understand their liabilities.

Obtaining data on all of these aspects of a business is vital to managing a complex business in a market environment. A CEO cannot manage a company without information that is accurate and up to date.

Investors also need access to this information. How can they make an intelligent decision regarding the prospects of a company unless they know its level of debt, its rate of growth, its overall expenses?

In the United States, all publicly traded companies must make this data available on a quarterly basis. Other countries have different reporting requirements and reporting periods. In the United States, the data must be audited by an independent accounting firm that attests to the information's correctness and validity.

By collecting company data as well as information on inflation, unemployment, business conditions, consumer confidence, and the plans of purchasing managers along with data on trade, savings levels, debt levels, and many other types of economic information, individuals can obtain a pretty good summary of how the economy is doing at any time. In the United States, most of this data is free or very inexpensive and available from the government and from private sources on the web, in newspapers, on TV, and in magazines. And, while the Soviets found they had a dearth of information, the United States has it in droves.

Even so, not everything is rosy.

While it is comforting to realize that you can get a hard drive full of data within seconds of its release, the problem is that because the economy is so complex, the data is not always meaningful or even accurate. If the data was meaningful and accurate, why would economists squabble so much in their forecast? Why would they debate so much over the exact date a recession begins or ends? And why would policy makers be in such a quandary with regard to whether a stimulus package will actually result in growth or simply more inflation?

The economy is complex, highly complex. Each moment of the day millions of transactions take place. Some of these are large; some, small. Some are complicated and some are simple. In a $10-trillion economy, keeping track of everything from the aggregate sales figures for airliners to aggregate sales figures for eyeliner is not easy.

That's the problem with economies—a big, vibrant one like ours or a dilapidated one like the Soviet Union used to have. Measuring anything that big is tricky and even the best economist or market analyst has to make inferences. And, while it is easy to find the length of the missing side of a right-angle triangle using the Pythagorean theorem, there are no Pythagorean theorems for deducing the future from inaccurate economic data. So what do great economists, investors, and observers do? They rely upon their experience to fill in the missing elements. What that means is that the great visionaries of commerce interpolate the future; they do not forecast the future.

By interpolating the future, I mean that the best investors first look at the GDP data and then ask themselves whether it makes sense when compared with other data that is already out there. Does a growing GDP seem like the right answer when unemployment is still rising? Does it seem reasonable when retail sales are down or consumer confidence lags? Can a barely growing GDP be sustained?

Using common sense to ascertain the veracity of just-released, often inaccurate data is tricky business. Perhaps a few legendary economists and investors could do it. But most people cannot. For them, unless the big-picture data can be viewed over a longer term, it just is not taken seriously. As a result, when I was writing about the markets, most economists and investors I would call upon would begin telling me about the future with the caveat that it is difficult to make any assertion about the future with just a single quarter's information. This is true for countries and it is true for companies.

And yet . . .

When new data is released—earnings from a company or GDP or inflation data for the country—it continues to be taken as true. As a result, each release of information moves the market. And, because it does, the savviest investors and observers understand the odd principle that while the new data is almost always inaccurate, it must be treated as if it were correct.

From the macro perspective, that's a problem for

investors. But it is also a problem for companies that make their plans based upon these figures. Big companies like IBM, Dell, Compaq, and Gateway (or GM, Ford, and DaimlerChrysler) create sales forecasts based on how well they think the overall economy will do based on the data that is released. They order parts and book factory time based on those estimates. They give those estimates to their sales teams and to their dealers. Everyone, from suppliers to retailers, falls in line.

Unlike the old Soviet-style economy, when a central planner in Moscow decided on when and on what to invest, the market system is far more fragmented, which means it is also more resilient. If either Dell or Gateway or IBM makes the wrong bet due to the data, chances are its rivals are making better bets. One manufacturer or insurer or airline may go bust, but there are others that can take up the slack. Not only are there other companies to take up the slack, there are other companies to purchase the assets when a company is defunct.

If you put this together, what becomes apparent is that the market triumphed over its rival non-market system, not so much because market participants are smarter or just because they have better information. Market economies triumphed for another reason. They are more decentralized and made up of smaller pieces. As a result, they are more fault tolerant. Having a single planner in Moscow do all the planning for an industry may gain efficiencies, but it also concentrates all of the risks for a sector in a single set of decisions. Since economic information is imperfect, it is much more prudent to build additional smaller companies, each with their own view of the world. If Compaq and Gateway were to make the wrong bet on the future, IBM and Dell might get it right. The overall system is safer, though the individual companies have a higher level of risk.

Even so, people can become pretty adept at reading the tea leaves on the macro basis by watching as many numbers as they can and keeping their own tallies. Aside from a few anomalous times—like the 1970s—you can spot a lot of economic problems just by looking, as Yogi Berra said.

In many ways, company data, even though it is audited, also requires interpolation and interpretation. An entire class of people—analysts—are charged with that responsibility, for good or ill.

A good deal of the blame for the run-up and bursting of the Internet bubble has been placed on stock market analysts. Equity analysts have been accused of hyping stocks in which they had invested and in which the companies that employed them had either interests or business relationships.

The story has been told many times that gullible investors bought billions of dollars' worth of shares in money-losing Internet companies on the advice of highly paid equity analysts. Analysts, the story goes, kept changing their mantra about what matters most in high-tech investing. From the standpoint of investors, the metrics were always changing. First, analysts said profits did not matter, but eyeballs (website viewers) did. Next the analysts said "click throughs" were what mattered, meaning the number of people who logged on and surfed through a site. After that, the analysts said revenue growth mattered, and finally—having come full circle—the analysts said profits mattered. At each stage in the four- to five-year Internet investment frenzy, the metrics that mattered changed. Suspicious investors believe that conflicts of interest among the analysts were responsible for these shifts.

The trouble is that while some analysts may have been guilty of over-hyping a stock, many other analysts were simply caught up in dot.com fever themselves. They were duped by the overblown rhetoric of the Internet, just as their clients were, and they believed what the dot.com CEOs said.

Even so, since early 2001, most reputable investment houses have put limits on their analysts' investments while requiring them to submit to greater disclosure regarding their own stock-ownership positions. No one knows for sure whether these rules go far enough.

Analysts are employed on Wall Street to make estimates of a company's revenue and earnings, determine its value, and compare its value with its price. These are the same functions performed by most good investors.

Analysts usually specialize by sector, but sectors are more difficult than ever to define. (What is GE? Is it a manufacturer? It is hard to say. GE derives most of its profits from its financial division, but most of its revenue from other types of operations, like plastics, manufacturing, and broadcasting. Similarly, Intel, the largest chip producer, is a big venture capital investor and also provides services. Boeing, the nation's largest defense and aircraft manufacturer, also sells computer services and has a big financial division.)

Analysts are supposed to study companies and report to investors on how those companies are doing. In the old days—that is, before 2001—managers of companies would often give their favorite analysts "whispered" estimates of a company's performance just before each quarterly announcement. Analysts, in turn, would pass those estimates along to their favored clients. Armed with early information on profitability and other factors before a formal release of data, an analyst's best clients would often buy or sell shares of a stock based on that information. It is easy to see why whispered estimates gave certain investors an unfair advantage. As a result, the SEC banned whispered estimates in 2001, though it is difficult to understand why it waited so long.

But while a couple of questionable practices of the analysts have ended, their role remains important due to their in-depth knowledge of the companies they cover. And yet, one big reason that we still need analysts has to do with the type of information that companies report.

For the most part, companies report quarterly on a very traditional set of indicators, which I previously mentioned in brief. The problem is that while these indicators explain how a company did *financially,* they do very little to explain how a company *will* do. One reason for that is because companies rarely report critical non-financial measures.

Here is what I mean.

Suppose you want to invest in a technology company like Intel that produces microchips for computers and other applications. To know whether that company is a really good bet for the future, you probably need to know a lot of things the company does not report. A lot of those items are not financial or are only indirectly financial. These non-financial items are the type of information that would be important to know if you were part of a company that is acquiring another company. As investors, few of us are acquiring an entire company. Even so, our judgment regarding where to invest would be better if we had access to more non-financial information and thought like acquirers.

If your company were to buy a chip-making company, you would want to know such things as how many of its chips were delivered but returned due to defects, how many new products are in the pipeline, whether customers are satisfied with the products, how many deliveries of its product are made on time. Information like this is available to an acquirer during the due diligence process.

In addition, if you were acquiring a chip company, you would want to know what percentage of sales comes from new products versus old products and whether that ratio is changing. You would also want to know whether the company was fully staffed or whether there were senior research or manufacturing positions that were vacant. You might also want to know how many customers the company has, whether sales growth has come from selling more to the same customers or from selling the same or less to additional customers. You might even want to know if the employees of the company felt satisfied in their jobs, or were unhappy.

Right now, the only way to find out that type of information is from equity analysts, although some corporations recognize that if they were to provide better non-financial information, they might be more successful in explaining their strategies to their investors and keeping their investors loyal when there is a minor setback. A number of people believe that stocks would be more accurately valued by the markets if the investment community had a better understanding of what drives their business. Volatility among certain stocks would fall. But until companies change the way they report, investors will be forced to rely on the insights of analysts.

Since prices are a form of information, markets react whenever there is new information. A disaster, a terrorist attack, a sudden economic setback: each affects the way a stock is priced.

For investors looking at the market, the best way to be prepared is to study the material that is available to them about the economy and about corporate performance. Almost every publicly traded company has a website and for each of these websites there are several run by the company's friends and foes. In addition, there are chat rooms on the web with a nearly endless stream of information about each major company. There are economic chat rooms and even economic chart rooms where data is displayed.*

By keeping up to date with the information that is released, investors have a better chance of determining value.

But the real magic of the markets is that while information is available freely, the interpretation of that information is distributed. Each market participant has within his or her mind a picture of reality that is shaped by each new input of data. When new figures are released on a macro or micro level, the actions they spark are uncoordinated and distributed, which, for the most part, spreads around the risk.

But one thing is certain when looking at market information. The caveats that all brokerages and fund managers are required to make by law—*that past performance is not a guarantee of future results*—is not an opinion but

---

*One of my favorite economic sites is run by Dr. Ed Yardeni at www.yardeni. com. It is a treasure trove of information.

a certainty. By definition, all prices are set when a transaction occurs, which means in the present, and each of these transactions determines the future. The past, while interesting, is in many ways superfluous. A company's heritage, its legendary leaders, its legacy of products mean very little when judged against the tough standards of tomorrow and tomorrow's competitors. And while each transaction is performed today, the market's lean is toward the future. Like the jaws of evolution that have devoured one species after another, the markets treat even their best and largest investors with the same cold logic. The only defense against the market's snap decisions on who will lose and who will win is to arm yourself with information. And, when it comes to information, more is always better than less.

CHAPTER NINE

The Market as Copilot

Mr. Market, as Warren Buffett calls the world's stock, bond, and currency markets, is a very rich fellow. In my mind, I see him as a cross between Mr. Peanut (dapper yet dignified) and the Monopoly Man (condescending, aloof, cold, self-absorbed, acquisitive).

If money is power, as the saying goes, Mr. Market is perhaps the world's most powerful chap. Not only is he sitting on a pile of cash, $20 trillion or more invested globally, he is also confidently waiting for trillions more to trickle into his markets from money on deposit in banks and in money market accounts. It is no wonder that James Carville, the consultant who ran the election and reelection campaigns for President Clinton, said he wanted to be reincarnated as the bond market—that's where the real power lies.

Because the markets are so big, they have transformed our lives. They have monetized almost everything, as previously noted. In practice that means that anything with value also has a price.

Consider, for a moment, David Bowie, the flamboyant British rocker from the '70s with a flair for business. Not only did he make a ton of money from his music with such album hits as *Space Oddity* and *Ziggy Stardust,* but in 1997, he took the projected future earning power from his catalog of songs and turned it into an issuance of bonds. The bonds, valued at $55 million, paid an interest rate of 7.9 percent over ten years. Bowie Bonds were rated by an independent rating agency and were purchased, *en masse,* by the Prudential Insurance Company of America, a group not normally associated with pierced belly buttons and tattoos. Bowie used some of the proceeds from the sale of his bonds to invest in other businesses, including a website. But the point is, he turned a static asset—a catalog of songs—into something dynamic, a bond. In the process he got $55 million, which will be paid back from future earnings. And—best of all—he still owns the songs. Other pop stars are now doing the same thing.

Turning a revenue stream, in this case from songs, into bonds or some other type of instrument is nothing new. Aircraft leases, car loans, and home mortgages have been turned into bonds—or bond equivalents—for years. But capitalizing on something as intangible as songs *is* something new. It represents a huge leap forward in financial creativity. Perhaps at some point gifted graduate students in genetics or physics will turn their future earning power into bonds. In that way, an investor could spot a sharp, newly minted Ph.D. from MIT or Harvard or Berkeley, give her a couple of million dollars, and have her pay it back from the proceeds of her career. If you bought enough of these, some would of course be duds, but some would pay off big-time.

WHAT THE MARKETS WANT

The markets are about ownership and credit and debt. Stocks are ownership claims and bonds are forms of credit and debt. All other financial products derive from these two fundamental concepts. But in some instances, as we shall see, the distinctions become blurred as the market *really* works wonders.

In most instances there are reasons, however, for favoring either a stock or bond investment as a buyer or a seller. Why, after all, didn't David Bowie create stock in David Bowie Inc., for example, and sell stock? Why did he raise money with bonds?

The main reason for the difference is that with stock (unlike bonds) a direct ownership stake is taken in the company. A say in governance goes along with that ownership stake. What happens is that by issuing stock, a company's founder is often bypassed. Governance is carried out by a board of directors whose principal job is to represent the interests of the company's shareholder groups. If David Bowie were to sell shares in David Bowie Inc., a board of directors representing shareholders could remove him from the job of CEO if they did not like the way he was running his company.

Many entrepreneurs and business owners are reluctant to give up that much control in exchange for investment cash. With bonds, an investor gets a claim on future earnings, but has hardly any say in how the company is run, unless the company verges on bankruptcy. Levi

Strauss, the longtime maker of Levi's brand jeans as well as other types of apparel, was a publicly traded company with a sizable portion of the shares owned by the descendants of the founder of the company. The family, which was wealthy and philanthropic, decided that rather than let its shareholders and board of directors dictate how the company was run, they would buy back all the shares and take Levi Strauss private. Later, when the privately held company needed cash, it issued bonds, not stock. By doing so, it could use some of its profits from the apparel business for its philanthropic activities without shareholders arguing that the money the company was giving away really belonged to them.

Stock and bond investors and issuers are seeking the same thing—to maximize income and minimize their risk. But they make their choices of a stock or bond because they are seeking different trade-offs on the risk/reward continuum.

With bonds, there is generally less risk than with stocks because investors have a claim on the issuing company's assets. In the eyes of the legal system, bond holders are viewed as creditors—similar to banks—and the company's assets are viewed as collateral. The power of bondholders does not rest in having a say in whether the CEO should be retained or fired. It rests in what might be called *the end of days*. When a company is really on the ropes—so much so that it may go bust—the creditors are brought in to meet with management about how they will get paid.

In practice, if the entity issuing Bowie Bonds—or any other type of bonds—went bankrupt, for example, the bondholders would be given a say in how the remaining assets of the issuing company were divvied up. If the company had real estate or machinery (or a catalog of songs!), those assets could be sold to pay off the bond-holders and other creditors. If any money was left, after the bondholders and other creditors were paid, that money might go to the stockholders.

Bonds are almost always issued by companies that have assets that can be sold. In the case of David Bowie, it is his music; in the case of United Airlines, it is its air-planes; in the case of a real estate company, it is its build-ings. The ability to foreclose on a company's underlying assets mitigates much of the risk associated with purchas-ing the bonds. In return for this protection against risk, bonds have less upside potential than stocks. Bowie Bonds, for example, will never be worth more than $55 million, plus interest. But their downside risk rarely reaches zero. When bonds are designed, there is usually sufficient leeway so that if the worst scenario occurred, the issuer could make good on most, if not all, of its obligations.

On the risk/reward continuum, stocks have almost no limit to their upside return. Shares of companies like GE, Berkshire Hathaway, Microsoft, Home Depot, and others that cost a hundred dollars or less when they were issued, might be worth thousands or even tens of thousands of dollars at their height, when adjusted for splits. But if the company issuing the stock goes bust, watch out. There is no limit to how fast the price of shares can fall—and they can fall to zero.

THE MARKETS HAVE CHANGED

In the old days, when shares were held by a few wealthy individuals with deep pockets, the Old Boys network worked wonders to keep governance issues from being talked about in public. Stockholders whispered to their brokers and brokers whispered to their friends on the board. In the days when Cadillac cars were the "Standard of the World" and a martini—not Evian—was the preferred lunchtime drink, insurance companies and large pension and retirement funds owned most of the shares. Today, the tables have turned with more than 60 percent of the nation's households owning stock.

In the old days, a CEO's tenure was usually as secure as a college professor's. Old Boy investors with seats on the board rarely voted to dislodge a country-club buddy from either the board or from senior management. If a company had a down year, the board and management attributed it to "business conditions"—whatever that means. It was rare for a board to expect managers to rise above those conditions.

But in the 1980s, when the markets really began to grow, something new occurred. Not only did Mr. Market become unimaginably rich—with $2 trillion invested at the beginning of the decade—much of that money became "self-directed," with companies creating 401(k) plans and other programs managed by employees themselves. With employees managing their own money, cash became far more mobile and began flooding into mutual funds. But when it came to individuals managing their own money, they were not content with low rates of return. They wanted performance. A new breed of performance-driven money manager began to emerge.

The 1980s was also the era that gave rise to what Michael Milken, the financier, called the "democratization of capital."

During this period, with trillions under management,

a new crew of investors emerged. Many of these investors had money from the pension funds of an entire state's population of government employees. California and New York had hundreds of billions of dollars under management. Most of this money was invested conservatively, but a small portion of it was placed with small private partnerships and investment funds that were going after big returns. Some of these small firms, like Kohlberg, Kravis, Roberts & Co.; Forstmann, Little; and Clayton, Dubilier and Rice used money from these funds, borrowed more from banks, and bought entire companies, rather than a few shares. Usually they bought companies that were under-performing or bloated with overhead. They pared down the cost structures of these companies, sold off divisions, and sold what was left in the public markets. Some of these firms produced huge returns for investors and—because they were buying entire companies—struck terror in the hearts of CEOs and managers.

One of the innovations of this era was the use of new types of vehicles for financing acquisitions. Principal among these tools was the so-called junk bond.

Junk bonds are bonds that are issued by companies that have a higher level of risk than blue chip companies and therefore pay a higher interest rate to borrow money. Sales of junk bonds had always occurred but there was no organized market for them and few people really gave them much thought.

But everything changed when Milken came up with a brilliant new way to view these bonds. Rather than thinking about them individually, Milken advocated thinking about junk bonds as portfolios of investments. Using an intricate mathematical model, Milken was able to construct for clients portfolios of bonds that paid high levels of return and overall were in some cases far less risky than low-yield blue chip bonds. By balancing one bond against another, even if one or two high-risk companies went bust, the remaining bonds in the portfolio paid off. In the '80s, *when some of these bonds were yielding 20 percent or more,* pension funds and other types of financial institutions used a portion of their funds to buy Milken's portfolios of bonds.

Attracted by the yields and the safety of these portfolios, within a short span of time, Milken created an ocean of investment capital from his offices in Beverly Hills. High-yield bonds, issued by companies emerging from bankruptcy or in difficult times, helped them heal. Once on their feet, they paid off handsomely.

Milken's real contribution was far greater than simply to sell portfolios of bonds. His real contribution was to get investors to understand that the stock and bond markets were not really separate markets. Instead, he got them to understand that the capital markets are a vast, single ocean with myriad bays and inlets and lagoons. Some of these lagoons were where bonds were devised, packaged, and sold. Others were where stocks were traded. At different times in the economic life of a company—or the economic life of the country—investors and funds-seekers would have to visit different areas of the ocean.

Milken worked closely with investors, devising their portfolios to mitigate long-term risks and maximize returns. But he also worked with the issuers of bonds to get them to create financing mechanisms and vehicles in advance of their needs. He even got companies to think about the tax implications of their financing in advance of what they would have to pay.

By viewing Mr. Market as a single pool with numerous specialized inlets, Milken was able to devise ways to finance nearly any corporate objective for nearly any client—big or small, old or new. Milken and his partners at Drexel Burnham Lambert, his firm, changed the shape of corporate America by financing and refinancing ailing companies with solid prospects for growth as well as funding friendly and hostile acquisitions. In his one-ocean worldview, Milken used bonds to buy stock and stock to repay bonds. The value of one could be exchanged for the value of the other as long as the price made sense.

While Milken has his share of detractors—for some he was the savior of the economy, to others he was the Lex Luthor of the economy—one thing is certain (at least to me): Milken created a tremendous pool of liquidity and guided its use with surgical precision. He did it in a way that took an often bloating and ailing American economy and made it lean, mean, and resilient. Much of the strength and resilience of the economy today—including its ability to rebound in times of adversity—is due to the way people using Milken's financing vehicles remade ailing companies or put their entrepreneurial zeal to work.

Although I am biased, I also believe the record of Milken's achievement is clear. He got people to think differently about the markets and to view them as one. And while academics may dispute his role, and others may argue he stepped over the legal line, his deeds really are his record. By using the markets in a more adroit fashion than had ever been done before, Milken created enormous wealth. A partial list of the companies he helped get started (or repaired) includes MCI (now MCI/Worldcom); News Corporation; Time Warner, Turner Broadcasting, CNN (now AOL Time Warner); CapCities ABC (now Disney); Mirage Resorts; Viacom; Holiday Inns; McCaw

Cellular, TCI, and Liberty (now all AT&T); Chrysler (now DaimlerChrysler); and many others.

So why mention this now?

WHO'S REALLY RUNNING THE SHOW?

The growth of the capital markets, combined with the innovations by Milken in the '80s, and others more recently, has shifted the balance of power. Companies are no longer run by a small group of well-heeled CEOs who pay little heed to the market. Instead, most CEOs I have met run their companies with one eye on their stock prices, real time. Some companies have screens throughout their offices and even factories showing stock prices for all employees to see. They do so with the aim of making certain that the value a company creates is consistent with the price of its shares. Sometimes it is difficult to get it right.

Creating value that is reflected in the price of a share has become so important that increasingly, CEOs have been dismissed by boards for failing to increase both value and price. This is particularly true when two companies merge or one company acquires another.

Take for example the case of DaimlerChrysler. When Daimler-Benz acquired (the press releases said it was not an acquisition but a merger of equals) Chrysler in 1998, it paid $36 billion and argued that by combining the two companies, there were ways to reduce costs and increase revenue by far. These synergies were large enough that it made more sense for Daimler to buy Chrysler than to invest the money in expanding its own operations. Over time, the companies would be worth far more as one, than if they had stayed on their own. At the time of the merger the combined value of the two companies was $92 billion.

But Mr. Market never warmed up to the idea and instead of bidding up the stock of the two companies, he pulled them down. A year after the merger, the value of the two companies had fallen to about $66 billion. Three years later the value of the combined companies had fallen from $43 billion to about $35 billion. In a little over three years, Mr. Market had become so turned off by the deal, that he set the price of the combined companies at less than the value of Chrysler alone. Or, seen from the other parties' perspective, in about three years, the merger had wiped out the entire going-into-the-deal value of Daimler-Benz—maker of Mercedes-Benz automobiles, trucks, and a host of other high-quality products. Rather than watch and wait, the DaimlerChrysler leadership in Germany dispatched a team to Detroit to fix the problems. Though it is still a work in progress, the power of the market proved to be a huge impetus to get the company to act. New products and new processes have been the result.

Sometimes Mr. Market is a forecasting genius—where money goes today, profits flow tomorrow. At other times he is subject to—how shall I say this?—delusion.

Consider these examples. For several years Mr. Market bid up the price of Internet stocks. At the time, so powerful and rich was he, that Mr. Market was not much different from his closest friend, the Emperor Who Wore No Clothes.

In 1999, at the height of the so-called New Economy and the Internet boom, Mr. Market smiled a naked smile and exuded self-confidence "I have seen the future and it is on the web," he said. In fact, everyone was saying it.

But the truly wacky character of Mr. Market's mind only became apparent later. Let's look at a few comparisons.

In 1999, at the height of the Internet boom, Cisco Systems, a high-quality producer of devices that support the infrastructure of the web, had revenues of about $13 billion and yet, *its market capitalization valued the company at $337 billion!* (Cisco's market capitalization actually climbed to about $500 billion briefly.) At the same moment, Yahoo!, an Internet company with sales of only $456 million, *had a market cap of $93 billion.*

As these companies were setting market capitalization records, consider how the so-called Old Economy was faring. GM, with revenues in 1999 of $177 billion—*that's $177 billion!*—had a value of only $46 billion, *half the market cap of Yahoo!* And if that was not enough, Ford, a solidly profitable and growing company with revenues of $126 billion, was worth only $60 billion, *about one sixth the value of Cisco.*

Yo! Mr. Market, is anybody home?

HOW MR. MARKET THINKS

An experiment I once read about made a fascinating point about IQ tests and group intelligence. The experiment showed that if students in a classroom took individual IQ tests, the average IQ score turned out to be 100, which is not surprising, given 100 is average. But if these students in a class were allowed to take the tests as a group, the group's IQ rose to be about 120. In other words individuals are as smart as they are but groups have the potential to be as smart as their smartest members.

I suggest that this appears *not* to be the case with markets.

In all humility, I suggest that with markets, the inverse of the classroom experiment is probably true. Markets just may move to the beat of their dumbest members. With markets, the milk sometimes rises to the top while the cream sinks to the bottom.

I do not mean to upset anyone reading these pages, but if you consider the way money moves, does it really make sense to assume that if Daimler and Chrysler merge, the result is a company worth one third the price of the two companies at the beginning of their alliance? Or, does it really make sense for the GM, *a massive global company with almost 350 times the revenue of Yahoo!,* to be worth half the value of the Yahoo! site?

In my view, despite a few academics who believe that markets are rational, markets are not rational. That does not mean that there are not some rational pockets hidden somewhere in the lagoons and inlets of the ocean. (Warren Buffett's gift seems to be that he has been able to latch on to a few.) But for the most part, markets shimmy and shake with every breeze that blows through the economy.

To really understand markets, and their power, it may be wise to study something like shamanism in addition to economics and finance. Shamanism, which uses all manner of techniques to intuitively arrive at a set of spiritual truths, at least came up with a few useful herbal medicines. As to the run-of-the-mill market prognosticators? I'm not so sure what they've come up with that's useful.

The way I view the market is that it is a very powerful tool for putting money in the hands of those who need it, particularly entrepreneurs. It is also a good way to raise cash to reinvest in companies that are attempting to snap back. Milken proved that this could be done. Markets are also an excellent way of spreading risks by divvying them up among a myriad of eager investors.

But with regard to the market's primary function—to set and constantly adjust prices—reality only goes to show that prices are not always subject to reason.

If the markets are a CEO's copilot, what are we to think? In 2001, in the aftermath of Mr. Market's dot.com madness, the market capitalization of Cisco was worth only $109 billion, although the company's revenues had nearly doubled to $22 billion. With that kind of performance, how do you evaluate the performance of the company's top team?

If you are an investor, you are obviously displeased. Cisco is worth less than a quarter of its value at its absolute top.

But if you are a customer, you are obviously pleased with the company as evidenced by the fact that you are buying twice as much stuff from it as when it was valued so highly.

The market really is fickle and there are only some things that business leaders can do to have it look their way. Some high-performing companies in sectors that are out of favor are like those clumps of kids at the high school dance—standing around, talking to themselves, not very popular. Other companies in sectors that are favored stand on the dance floor surrounded by would-be partners. And, while it is easy to move from the latter group to the former, it takes more than good hair and an little bit of *cool* to move from the former to the latter. For this reason, Milken once told me, companies should dip into the capital markets not when they need the money, but when the conditions are ripe.

And for investors, what is the corollary?

Don't go with the favored sector of the month. Instead, try to do what Buffett does and look for those rare pockets of reason in that fickle sea of foolishness.

Index

About the Author

Joel Kurtzman has been a reporter, editor, and columnist at the *New York Times;* the editor of the *Harvard Business Review;* and the founding editor of *Strategy and Business.* As a consultant, he has advised some of the largest companies in the world. He is currently the global lead partner for thought leadership and innovation at one of the largest consulting and accounting firms in the world. He is the author of *Thought Leaders: Insights on the Future of Business; The Death of Money: How the Electric Economy Has Destabilized the World's Markets and Created Economic Chaos; The Decline and Crash of the American Economy;* and fourteen other books. He has lectured extensively around the world.